silver surfers'

COLOUR GUIDE TO

THE internet

helen brookes

D1059009

004.678
BRO

foulsham
LONDON • NEW YORK • TORONTO • SYDNEY

foulsham

The Publishing House, Bennetts Close, Cippenham, Slough,
Berkshire, SL1 5AP, England

Foulsham books can be found in all good bookshops or direct from
www.foulsham.com

ISBN 0-572-03125-4

Cover photograph by Superstock

A CIP record for this book is available from the British Library.

Printed in Malaysia

Contents

Introduction

Welcome to the exciting world of the world wide web, the information superhighway, cyberspace, the net. Whatever you choose to call it, the internet has something for everybody – and that includes you.

But while the youngsters are so used to computers they seem to know what to do without even thinking about it, those who are more used to books and paper are often a bit nervous of having a go, and feel intimidated by the whole thing.

What's in this book?

The aim of this book is to cure you of that nervousness and give you a simple, step-by-step guide to getting started on the internet to find information you want, and show you how to send and receive e-mails.

- We'll just give you the information you need when you need it.
- We'll avoid unnecessary jargon.
- We'll target the practical things you want to achieve on the net so you can make things happen from day one.
- And you can take everything at your own pace, a piece at a time, so you really understand what you are doing.

If you already have a computer, just skip straight to the chapter you need and make a start. If you are dreading that first trip to the computer superstore, you'll find all the information you need to make a choice in Chapter 1 and we show you how to set it all up in Chapter 2.

Once you are off and running, we can guarantee there'll be no stopping you. There is so much just waiting to be discovered in cyberspace; the skills you learn in this little book could change your life in ways you can't even imagine!

Don't worry

Throughout the book, you'll find these 'Don't worry' boxes. They reassure you about things or explain extra bits and pieces you are likely to come across, but are not essential to understand at that stage. Just ignore them unless something is bothering you, or until you are comfortable with what you are doing and want to go back over them. Remember, you can go at your own pace!

What is the web?

The 'web', the 'world wide web', the 'net', the 'internet' all mean the same thing. They are just various names for all the millions of computers connected together across the world in a huge global network.

You become a part of this network when you get your own connection to the internet. Since the basic purpose of the web is to share information, once you are part of it you can then access information from anywhere in that global network or pass on information to someone else on the net.

Don't worry **about security**

This does NOT mean that just anyone has access to your computer once you link into the net; you are in control of the information you receive and the information you pass on. You do need to apply some commonsense security rules, but we'll talk about them on page 40.

Let's explain a few words you need to know

There's no getting away from the need to understand a few basic terms, as it will instantly make everything much clearer for you. If you were showing a Martian round your local library, you'd need to explain 'shelf', 'library card', 'catalogue', 'bar code' and 'alphabetical order' before you stood a chance of explaining the system. This is no different. So don't be put off – it really will make things simpler, and we'll keep up the library analogy to help you understand.

PC: This just means personal computer.

Apple: Apple, AppleMac, iMac – it's all the same for your purposes – are computers that do things in a slightly different way from a PC but what happens inside the computer makes no difference to you. You'll find a few things are different – some buttons may be in different places on the screen, for example – but the end results are just the same.

Online: You are online when you are connected to the internet – or in the e-library.

Web: As I said, this is the global network of computers sharing information. It means the same as: world wide web, net, internet, cyberspace. This is the e-library.

Website: Websites are the e-books; each one is a place where you look to find a specific type of information. It's also shortened to 'site'.

Web pages: Just like the pages of a book, a website can have as many pages as the creator wants to include. You can move around the pages in any order you like, plus you will probably have shortcuts (called links or hyperlinks) between some of the pages to help you move around the website – a bit like Snakes and Ladders.

Surfing: When you are visiting various websites and moving around the net, you are surfing. It's just wandering around the e-library to find information.

Who else is on the net?

The answer to this question is: most people! Individuals like you are part of the net when they go online to visit various websites.

Websites are created by various people: from individuals with special interests to educational or governmental institutions providing information, and businesses with commercial interests trying to sell you things. Anyone, including you, can create a web page that other internet surfers can visit.

What can I gain from being online?

One of the biggest benefits of being online is the amount of information that you have access to. The internet is infinitely bigger than any public library you ever visited – in fact, it's as big as all the libraries in the world. You will be able to find information on just about every subject from health and fitness to hobbies and holidays.

Don't worry **about misinformation**

Of course, the fact that anyone can set up a site means the internet does have its share of *mis*information. We'll give you some simple tips on how to find the good stuff and avoid the not so good, and your confidence and ability in making choices on credible websites will rapidly improve with practice.

The internet greatly increases the number of people you can get in touch with quickly and easily. There are dozens of ways you can communicate with like-minded people online, and you will learn how to use a number of these later in the book.

One more benefit of being online worth a mention has to be the ease and convenience that using the internet brings to day-to-day activities. Shopping, banking, paying bills, even planning and paying for holidays, can all be done online, saving you the hassle of doing business on the high street.

Finally, of course, you can do all of this any time of the day or night from the comfort of your own home

The ease and convenience of using the internet for everyday tasks, as well as the vast amount of information surfing brings within your reach, can make using the internet a really life-enhancing experience. The sooner you make a start, the sooner this book will be your gateway to this very exciting new world.

Chapter 1

Which Computer Should I Buy?

If you go to any computer store, you'll be confronted by a huge array of computers, all with different and very confusing specifications for things you may never have heard of. You don't have to worry about it!

If you went into a shop to buy a pair of size 7, brown lace-up shoes, you wouldn't spare a thought for the thousands of other shoes on display. This is no different. You just need to do a bit of homework in order to decide what you want before you go. You'll also find that most stores are sensible enough to sell computers as a package at a single price that includes everything you need. If you are new to computers, that's what to look for.

When you are buying a computer, two key factors affect how well it will work:

- how fast it can process information;

- how much data it can store.

The other crucial factor, of course, is:

- how much you want to spend.

In this chapter, we'll give you just enough information to help you understand the factors you need to take into account so you can choose a computer that will do everything you need it to do.

Which bit is the computer?

A computer is not just one piece of equipment, it's several bits linked together. All the parts of a computer you can see or touch are called the hardware.

Source: ImagExtra (www.andyjonesdesign.co.uk/imagextra)

The various parts you need when you buy a computer are:

- the monitor;
- the processor;
- the keyboard;
- the mouse;
- the printer.

The monitor

The most prominent part is the monitor, or screen, which looks like a TV screen. This is not the actual computer that does the work, it's just the screen on which everything is displayed.

Don't worry **about flat screens**

Most monitors are large. If you want to pay more, you can get a flat screen. It's just the same but takes up a lot less space. It does cost more, but prices are coming down all the time.

The processor

The working part of the computer is housed in a plastic or metal box. Some are flat and sit on the desk – which is why they are called desktop computers; some are tall and thin and stand on the floor under the desk, and these are sometimes called towers.

Don't worry **about iMacs**

If you choose an iMac, the processor and the monitor are all in one. There's more on iMacs on page 23.

The keyboard

The keyboard looks and works like a typewriter, and allows you to type letters and numbers that appear on the screen.

The mouse

The mouse is the small oval device with two buttons at the top and a central scrolling button. You use it to send instructions

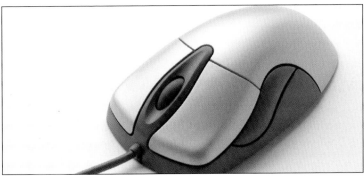

Source: ImagExtra (www.andyjonesdesign.co.uk/imagextra)

to the computer. When you move the mouse on your desk, it controls a cursor on the screen, so you can point your cursor to special characters on the screen and press the left button on the mouse to take you where you want to go. This is called pointing and clicking, a skill you will learn to perfect as you go along.

Don't worry **about the mouse with an iMac**

If you have an iMac, there won't be any buttons on your mouse.

Don't worry **about laptops**

Laptop computers – also called notebooks – are designed so you can carry them around, so everything – processor, screen, keyboard and mouse – fits inside the folding case. They are therefore much smaller than PCs in size but not in capability, and they are generally more expensive. Unless you are planning to keep moving your computer, or you are seriously short of space, stick with a PC.

Source: ImagExtra (www.andyjonesdesign.co.uk/imagextra)

The printer

Most computer packages come with an inkjet printer, so called because ink is sprayed on to the paper through tiny jets. Inkjet printers are suitable for most home printing. The quality does vary depending on how much you spend, but top-of-the-range inkjet printers can produce very high quality prints, such as brochures and photos.

Don't worry **about laser printers**

Laser printers are faster but are really only suitable for high-volume printing, say tens or even hundreds of pages a month.

What's inside the box?

If you are buying a car, you need to know about its engine capacity, petrol consumption, how much space there is in the boot and so on, so you can choose the right one for your individual needs.

When you are shopping for a computer package, you will need to look at the computer specifications listed as part of the marketing material. Once we've broken it down and explained what you need to know, it won't look so off-putting.

This is what it might look like:

Specification

- Intel Celeron processor 2.4GHz
- XP home operating system
- 40GB hard disk capacity
- 128MB RAM
- DVD-ROM and DVD-RW drive
- 15 in flat panel monitor
- 2 USB ports

Extras

- All-in-one printer, scanner, copier
- Digital camera
- Speakers

Internet ready

- Outlook Express
- Internet Explorer

Warranty

- One-year free warranty

Support and services

- Free home delivery and set-up
- Premium-line telephone support
- Free repairs or replacement
- Guaranteed discount for upgrades

What does the specification mean?

We'll go through the list one thing at a time so you know what to look for when you are shopping for your perfect package.

How fast does it run?

The computer's 'brain' is called a processor. The more powerful the processor, the better and faster the computer runs.

The bit of the list that mentions Megahertz (MHz) or Gigahertz (GHz) tells you the size of the processor; a thousand megabytes creates a single gigabyte. For most computer packages, speeds range from 366MHz to about 1200MHz. For basic internet surfing, printing photos and e-mailing, 366MHz is plenty but if you get more, that's good.

Is it up to date?

The system the computer uses to do its job is called the operating system. This is a program that organises everything that goes on inside the computer. Do not worry about the operating system as it will just run quietly in the background. MS Windows is the most common and, as you might expect, the computer companies are constantly updating the programs, so ideally buy the latest one. At the end of 2005, this is XP.

How much can it store?

Hard disk capacity tells you how much information the computer can store. This is measured in Gigabytes (GB). Letters and e-mails need relatively little storage space – for example, it would take 200 copies of the Bible to fill one Gigabyte of hard disk space. Graphics and music files tend to take up more room.

Modern PCs come with masses of hard disk space, usually starting at well above 10 GB. Unless you plan to store loads of movies or music, you are unlikely to run out of the hard disk space that comes with a regular PC.

How many things can it do at once?

RAM stands for Random Access Memory. This indicates how many documents and programs a computer can have open and running at the same time without it freezing up. RAM is measured in Megabytes (MB). For most internet-related tasks, 128MB is usually enough, but more is always better, so always go for more RAM if you can, especially if the price of the computer is not too affected by this specification.

What's the screen like?

A basic screen size is 15 in/35 cm, which is fine for what you need, but if you have space and the package offers a 17 in/ 43 cm or 19 in/48 cm monitor, go for it! We've already said that a flat screen takes much less space but costs more money Do consider it if space is an issue for you.

What do DVD-ROM and DVD-RW mean?

Most computers have a drive that allows you to play DVDs and computer games – that's the DVD-ROM part.

DVD-RW means you can copy to DVDs; this is not essential. You do want a CD-RW, though, which means you can copy information on to a CD.

If I don't sail, do I need a USB port?

This is simply the latest type of plug-in connection, which you will need to plug in your computer accessories, such as printers or scanners. Four is now usual: more is good. Don't worry if your PC seems to have fewer USB ports than you might need. It is unlikely you'll be using all your extras at once, and you can always share ports by swapping these around. You can also buy a 'hub', just like an extension socket, if you need one.

More than one plug

You'll have more than one electricity plug for your computer so it might be worth buying a four-way extension socket. Buy one with a surge protector.

Which extras do I need?

Most computer packages come with some optional extras. You will need to decide whether these are worth any extra cost. If they don't add to the overall cost and you are getting what you want, go for it!

All-in-one printer, scanner, copier: We have already said that most packages come with an inkjet printer. If you want to print out photographs, ask for photo quality; you get what you pay for, so it may be worth paying a little more for a good printer.

Most printers have two ink cartridges: one for black, plus one for the colours. More expensive printers have one for each colour. Check the price and availability of the cartridge refills.

Scanners are used to create electronic copies of documents, which can then be e-mailed, copied or stored on your computer. They are useful if you have a print you want to e-mail to your daughter, for example.

Courtesy: pixmania.co.uk

Modern printers often do both printing and scanning, so take up much less space and are very convenient.

Digital camera: A camera in a computer package is usually a fairly basic digital camera, so the picture quality is not as good as you might get from a normal camera. However, you can use it to take pictures to save on the computer, then e-mail to family or friends.

Courtesy: pixmania.co.uk

Web cam: Web cams are brilliant if you have grandchildren and would love to watch them show off a new toy or game! You can use a web cam to take video images to send over the internet in real time, turning your PC into a kind of video phone.

Speakers: Most PCs come with in-built microphones and speakers, but external speakers give better sound quality.

Source: ImagExtra (www.andyjonesdesign.co.uk/imagextra)

Internet ready

The 'hardware' is the computer itself; the 'software' is the programs that do the jobs you want it to do.

We've already met the operating system, which is a software program.

The ones you are interested in are the programs that help you do specific jobs on the computer, such as write a letter or send an e-mail. Because this is a book about using the internet, we'll limit ourselves to only the applications you will need for your internet tasks.

The most common program for e-mail is Outlook Express. The most common program for using the internet is Internet Explorer. You should have both these, or an equivalent, on your computer.

Anything else?

Occasionally, you'll find you need to buy an extra cable to connect everything together. Just ask your supplier if you need anything else and they'll tell you what you should buy.

It is also a good idea if your computer has an anti-virus program (see page 42).

Don't worry **about other software**

Your computer should also have various programs so you can write letters, work out finances or do other tasks, should you want to.

Instructions, warranty and after-sales service

Warranties and after-sales service do vary, so the best thing to do would be to ask your friends, relatives and colleagues about their experiences with various computer suppliers and base your decision on their recommendations. Generally speaking, you are best to opt for a reputable local supplier so you can contact them easily if you need help or support. As with any major purchase, check you are getting a good deal, get any assurances in writing and read the small print.

Every computer package will come with an instruction book that will show you how to set up and use the computer. Set-up instructions are usually good, but unfortunately the books are usually written by people who understand computers, so they can get a bit complicated. However, this book will get you well under way with basic tasks, by which time you can approach them with more confidence.

If the computer store offers a service where it delivers and sets up the computer at home for you, it might be a good idea to opt for this so you can skip the next chapter. Ask how much it will cost, and you will know whether it is worth it to you for convenience and peace of mind.

Modern computers are increasingly reliable, so hopefully you won't run into problems, but you get at least a year's guarantee. Be wary of paying extra for extended guarantees with too many get-out clauses; they might be useless should you run into problems.

Find out whether the shop has a helpline you can call in case you run into problems. Ask how much calls to the help centre cost, as they can be at premium rates.

After sales – what to look out for

- Home set-up service

- Customer helpline: how much does it cost to call per minute and how quickly can you get help? Check that they pick up the phone at all!

- PC repair service – availability, where the centre is local, etc.

- Returns policy – under what conditions can you get an exchange or refund?

Your reminder box

- Your best option is probably to buy an internet-ready package; take advice on what you need, depending on what you want to use your computer for.

- You will   need: a monitor, a processor, a keyboard, a mouse.

- You will probably want: a printer.

- You may want: a scanner, separate speakers.

- The MHz or GHz tells you how fast it can work.

- The GB tells you how much it can store.

- The RAM MB tells you how many things it can do at once.

- Look out for affordable support lines.

PC or Mac?

'The Mac' is a popular model of computer by Apple Computer Inc., a company founded in 1976 by Steve Jobs, Steve Wozniak and an Atari engineer named Ronald Wayne. The company's first product was Wozniak's computer, the Apple I. The Mac, short for Macintosh, was introduced in 1984. Apple computers were amongst the first to introduce the use of windows, icons and a mouse, making computing more user-friendly.

The Mac versus PC debate is generally a matter of personal taste. General opinion is that PCs are cheaper to own, having lower prices and, with a larger number of personnel familiar with PC components, easier to repair than Macs, which have to be returned to an authorised Apple dealer for repairs.

Apple, however, seems to have gained a good reputation for the stability of its operating system, but Microsoft is also getting good reviews of newer versions of its Windows operating system. In terms of programs and other software, Macs do come with some good and powerful applications, but you get a wider selection with PCs as most software writers concentrate their efforts on applications for Windows-based PCs. This does have its downside, however, as more viruses, spam, pop-ups and other irritants are also developed for PCs than Macs.

So what does this mean for the Silver Surfer? Most browsers run well on both computing platforms, and, once you start to surf, the differences between the two become very subtle, and can be ignored.

Here are a few differences in how the two computers work

	PC	Mac
Powering up computer	Press power button on processor chassis	Press power button on keyboard or monitor
Starting a program	Click on option for application from Program Menu found under the Start button on bottom left of desktop	Click on option for application from Menu found under Apple icon on top left corner of desktop
Closing a program	Click Exit option from File Menu	Click Quit option from File Menu
Shutting down the computer	Click on the Start Button then select Shut Down	Click the Special Menu and then select Shut Down

Chapter 2

Now I've Got It Home

If the computer shop offers a service where it also sets up the computer for you, by all means take it. It is the simplest way of getting started. However, if your computer arrives in what looks like dozens of different parts, do not feel too intimidated. This chapter will help you set it all up.

The best thing about this task is the fact that all computer parts fit together like a jigsaw puzzle, with every part fitting exactly into the slot it is meant for. When it comes to cabling up, pins go into holes and connectors' shapes always match. If the part does not fit, it does not belong. It is as simple as that. Most connections are also colour-coded, so the green pin goes into the green hole, and so on. This makes it difficult to get it wrong. If you find yourself forcing a connection, you probably need to take a second look at the instructions.

If you've ever put together a piece of flat-pack furniture, you are more than a match for this.

What to plug in where

Decide where you want to set up your workstation and you are ready to get started. You need to be near enough to an electricity socket and a telephone point. Get out the instruction sheet, which will give you a simple diagram of all the bits you should have.

The first thing to put in place is the base unit. If it is a tower, it is usually placed on the floor under your desk. The monitor should be positioned so that you feel comfortable when sitting facing it. If you have a flat base unit, you may want to put it on the desk underneath the monitor. Place the keyboard in front of the screen with the mouse to its right, if you are right-handed, or to the left if you are left-handed.

Plug in the monitor

This is your first task, and is easier than it looks as you only need to make one connection: from the monitor to the back of the base unit. The connecting cable for this comes attached to the monitor, and it is easy to tell where it needs to go – find the only socket on the base unit that matches the connector at the end of the monitor cable. Believe me, the only shapes that match are the correct ones! Don't force anything, make sure that pins correspond to holes and you'll be fine.

Plug in the keyboard and the mouse

Next you need to plug the keyboard into the base unit. Again, study the shape of the connector at the end of the cable attached to the keyboard. Match it to the corresponding plug on the back of the base unit and plug it in.

Now do the same with the mouse.

Because keyboard and mouse connectors are sometimes identical, there is a possibility you could plug them in the wrong way. Most base units will have a label on the plug so you know what goes where. Do not worry if you get these two in the wrong way round. No harm is done. All that would happen is that when you switch on the PC for the first time, a message will show up on the screen saying that the keyboard and mouse have been incorrectly plugged in. If this happens, just switch off the PC and swap the two connections. Done!

Plug in the power cables

The power cables come last. Make sure that you have cables that match the UK domestic power voltages.

Connect one end of the relevant power cable to the monitor and the other end to the power socket on your wall (or whatever power point you are using).

Connect one end of the relevant power cable to the base unit and the other to the power socket.

Don't worry **about the accessories**

If you have any accessories, such as a web cam or printer, these will come with separate instructions for setting them up and you can connect them later, once the PC has been set up.

You are ready to switch on

You are now ready to switch on the power to your PC. Turn on the power for both the monitor and the base unit on the power socket on your wall.

Press the on/off button on the computer. With a lot of clicking, whirring and blinking of lights, your computer comes to life for the first time. If any instructions come up on the screen, follow them to create initial settings such as giving your computer a name or setting up passwords. Eventually you will see the Microsoft Windows desktop.

There are now a few more terms you need to learn to make life easier:

Desktop: This is the screen that appears when you start up your computer and, just like a real desktop, is the starting point from which you can open various computer programs or view documents.

Icon: An icon is a tiny picture on your screen that represents a document, a program or a command. Clicking on the icon starts the application, opens the document or activates the command it represents.

Menu: This is just a list from which you choose whichever item you want.

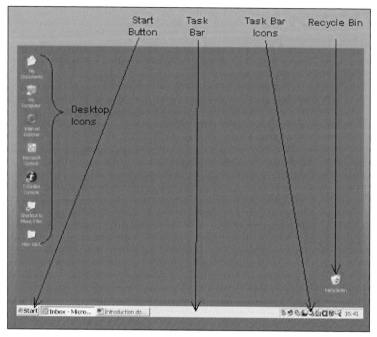

You also need to learn to use your mouse.

When you move your mouse, a pointer on the PC screen also moves, mimicking the movements you make on your desk. Move your mouse so that the pointer rests on any object on the computer screen. This is called pointing.

The mouse has three buttons on it: one on the left and the other on the right and a scroll button in the middle.

If you press once on the left button and let go, this is called clicking.

If you press and release the left-hand button quickly twice, that is a double-click.

The right-hand button opens more possibilities that you can take on when you are more familiar with working with the computer.

We'll tell you about the scroll button on page 51.

Connecting to the internet

Once your PC is set up and running, you need to decide how you will get connected to the internet. This is usually done via your telephone line. There are two ways to do this:

- a dial-up connection;
- a broadband connection.

Dial-up connections

You have bought an internet-ready PC, which means it already contains an internal modem, which is a device that allows you to send computer data over your telephone line. To use a dial-up internet service, you will need to connect your computer to your telephone wall socket using the cable supplied.

The disadvantages of using a modem connection are:

- they are slower than broadband so it takes longer to do anything online;
- you cannot make or receive telephone calls while you are on the net;
- you may not get online the first time you dial if lines are busy.

On the other hand:

- anyone with a phone line can use one;
- if you've never used broadband anyway, you won't be used to how fast that is – and dial-up is not that slow;
- you can use your mobile and sign up to 1571 so people can leave a message if you are online;
- it's only rarely that you don't get online first time.

If you really find you need your phone line or your internet connection on all the time, it's much better to go broadband than consider putting in another telephone line.

Broadband

The next option is broadband internet connection via your phone line. Broadband speeds are much faster than dial-up and you can still use your telephone to receive and make telephone calls while surfing.

All this clearly makes broadband a better choice for regular surfers, but there is one major drawback: not all telephone lines can support this technology. Before ordering a broadband internet connection, you need to check that your area has broadband availability. This checking service is offered by all broadband internet service providers who will run a quick check based on your postcode.

Broadband also uses a different modem, and this will either be installed for you or sent to you so you can do it yourself (although that's not a big deal).

Choosing an internet service provider

When you go online, you don't connect your computer directly with all the other computers out there. You sign up with what's called an internet service provider (ISP) who gives you access to the internet for a fee or for a small charge.

Connection and payment options

There are basically three options.

Pay as you go: 'Free' ISPs do not charge for connecting you to the internet, but every time you connect to the internet your telephone company will charge you for the cost of the telephone call for every minute you spend online. Although the telephone call remains local regardless of what website in the world you visit, the costs could add up considerably if you spend a lot of time online. This option is therefore only suitable for people who go online only occasionally.

Unmetered access: The charge for this type of connection option remains fixed regardless of how much time you spend online in a month, day or night, and you pay a fixed fee, usually by direct debit. This payment option is more suitable for people who plan to spend a lot of time online. A cheaper variant of this connection type is one that allows unmetered access during evenings and weekends only.

Tips for selecting a dial-up ISP

Services are generally quite similar, so go for a reputable name, and ask someone you know if they are happy with the service they get.

Charges: Check the monthly amount you will pay.

Telephone charges for technical support: See if they have telephone support and find out how much it costs. Charges to some support lines can be prohibitive, costing 50p or more per minute. Shop around; ISPs with local call charges for support do exist.

Session limits for unmetered access: Unlimited access does not always mean that. Some ISPs limit the total number of hours you can have online per month.

Minimum contract period: Some ISPs tie you in for a minimum period of six months or a year. Shop around for contracts you can terminate without too much fuss should you need to.

Broadband: Broadband internet connections are 'always on' so the amount you pay per month will always be fixed. How much you pay depends on the speed of the connection. The slowest connection speed is 256K, which is roughly five times the speed of a good dial-up service; if you are going broadband, it's probably worth going for the option that is ten times faster. Some broadband ISPs bundle in other services such as digital TV, so shop around to see what is best for you.

Tips for selecting a broadband ISP

Download limits: Some ISPs limit how much information you can download off the net on to your computer. You can get unlimited 'download'.

Connection fees: Some ISPs do not charge for the cost of the broadband modem and initial connection. Generally speaking, if you go for the faster packages costing more each month, you won't have to pay any upfront costs.

Bandwidth: This is just a measure of your connection speed, so how fast the connection will work. You will generally pay more for faster access speeds.

Signing up and getting online

Once you've decided which ISP you will use, getting online is easy. The instructions for setting up your connection are shown below if you need them, but most ISPs will give you software on a CD – you'll have seen the CDs by the checkouts in all the supermarkets and computer stores – that automates the process.

Broadband ISPs will send you a connection pack through the post, which will include an external broadband modem, appropriate cables, software and connection instructions.

If you have to set up the connection manually, follow the instructions starting on page 33.

To close a window

Just click on the little cross in the top right-hand corner.

Connecting to the internet with a CD

If you have a CD from your ISP – such as tiscali, aol, btinternet or demon – all you need do is insert the CD into your computer's CD drive. Wait a few moments and a window will open on the screen. Follow the instructions it gives you, then click on Next. It will guide you step by step through the process.

Connecting to the internet if you don't have a CD

When you sign up for the service, your ISP provides you with a:

- telephone number to dial;

- username;

- password.

When prompted for this information during the set-up process, it is important, especially with passwords, to type in the characters exactly as they appear in the documentation you get, as it could be important to use capital letters in the right place (they might tell you that the text is 'case sensitive'.)

Step 1

1. Click once on the **Start** button on the Windows desktop to open the **Program Menu**.

2. From the Program Menu, click once on the **Connect To** option.

3. On the sub-menu that appears, find the **Show all connections** option and click on it once to open the **Network Connections** window.

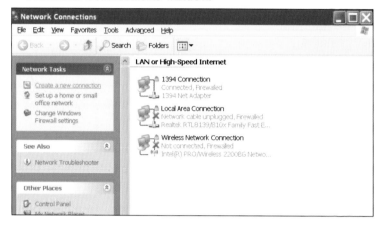

Step 2

1. On the top left-hand side of the window, find **Create a new connection** and click once on it to open the **New Connection** wizard.

2. A 'wizard' describes a small program with a series of instructions that guide you through a task. Each window of the wizard gives you a list of options to choose to complete the task.

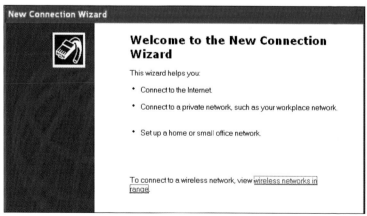

3. Click once on the **Next** button to start the wizard.

4. The **Network Connection Type** window appears.

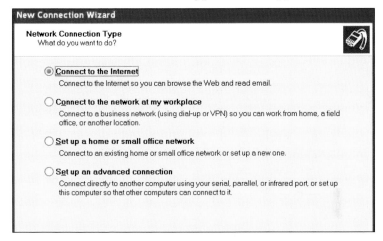

Step 3

1. Make sure the **Connect to the Internet** option is selected. If not, click once in the small circle next to it to select this option.

2. Click on the **Next** button to continue.

3. The **Getting Ready** window appears.

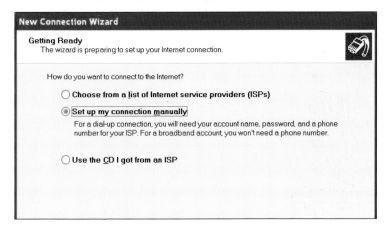

Step 4

1. Select **Set up my connection** manually by clicking once on the small circle next to this option.

2. Again, click **Next** to continue.

3. The **Internet Connection** window appears.

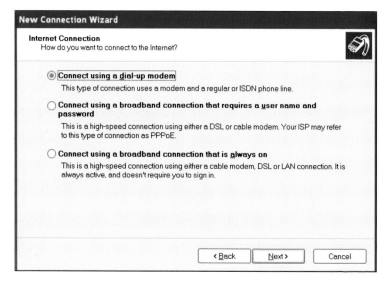

Step 5

1. In this window, make the appropriate selection for your connection service, and click **Next** to move to the **Connection Name** window.

2. Type in a name for the connection (e.g., a shortened version of your ISP's name).

3. Click once on the **Next** button to move to the next window.

4. For dial-up connections you will be taken to the **Phone Number to Dial** window. Type in the number supplied by your ISP.

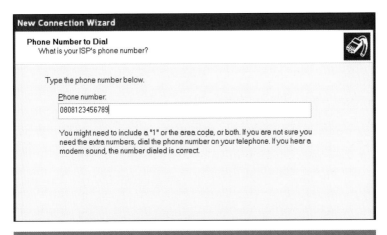

Step 6

1. If the **Connection Availability** window appears, just click the **Next** button to accept the default settings.

2. This takes you to the **Internet Account Information** window.

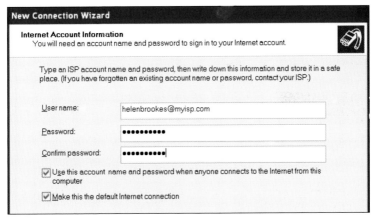

3. Type in your username and password.

4. Notice the boxes at the bottom of the window. Unless your ISP has instructed otherwise, it is a good idea to make sure a tick appears in all these boxes so that the options next to them are selected.

5. Click **Next** to continue. The final window appears.

Step 7

1. To complete this task, click once in the box labelled **Add A New Shortcut To My Desktop**. This places an icon on your desktop from which you can start the program that will connect you to the internet.

2. Click once on the **Finish** button to complete this task.

3. The wizard disappears and is replaced by the **Connect** window.

4. You may now connect to the internet straight away by clicking once on the **Dial** button.

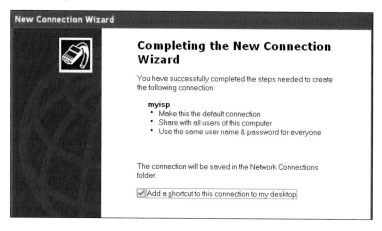

Making your first dial-up connection

1. To connect to the internet, find the icon that you created in Step 7 of the last exercise on your Desktop. It will have the name of your ISP.

2. Double-click it. The dialler window opens. Notice how your password remains undisplayed.

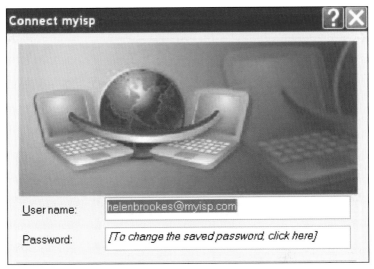

Connect myisp [?][X]

| User name: | helenbrookes@myisp.com |
| Password: | *[To change the saved password, click here]* |

3. Click once on the **Dial** button. That's it!

4. In a short while, a small window appears confirming that you've been successfully connected. You will learn how to surf, use e-mail and perform other online tasks in subsequent chapters.

Your reminder box

- If you are not confident about setting up your PC, arrange for the store engineer to do it for you.

- Choose **broadband** for faster internet access and to be able to use your phone and computer at the same time.

- A **dial-up** connection is cheaper but slower.

- Learn one computer term each day to make it easier to understand computer instructions.

- Follow the tips on page 30 to choose your **ISP**.

- Sign up to a service that suits your needs.

Chapter 3

A Word About Security

The internet is no different from the high street: the vast majority of people are honest and law-abiding and a few are not. You therefore need to take a few sensible precautions against those who don't have your best interests at heart.

It is an unfortunate fact that the internet community includes individuals, called hackers, who try to gain unauthorised access to computers connected to the internet. Attacks can range from the simply irritating to the serious, where your computer documents could be stolen or corrupted. Broadband users are at slightly more risk because their internet connection is always on and connection speeds are faster.

To minimise risk:

• Switch off your connection when you have finished using the computer.

• If you're on broadband, switch off the computer when you're not using it.

This chapter is not meant to frighten you or put you off getting on to the net. You can protect yourself quite easily by taking a few commonsense precautions. Firstly, you can set up some protective measures before you start. Secondly, you can follow some straightforward rules when you are surfing.

The next words you need to know

Download: This simply means copying something from the internet to your computer.

Upload: Not surprisingly, this means copying something from your computer to somewhere else on the net.

Firewalls

A firewall prevents unauthorised access to your PC by monitoring anyone trying to make a connection from the internet to your PC and checking whether or not they are legitimate. Any suspicious connections are blocked.

When setting up your connection to the internet, ask your ISP to include a firewall. If you did not do this at the start, don't worry. Just give them a call and ask if they can set up a firewall.

If they don't supply one, you could buy a commercial one from your computer shop. Tell them how you use your computer and how much you want to spend and they will be able to advise you as to which one is best for you.

• **Software**: Firewall software is a program on a CD. You put the CD in the CD drive and a wizard – step-by-step instructions – will tell you how to install it.

• **Hardware**: This comes in a box that sits between your computer and internet connection to intercept physically and then scrutinise any data going to and coming from the internet.

Anti-virus and spyware programs

Sometimes, even with the best of precautions, some unwanted programs do make their way into your PC. Programs created to prevent you using your computer properly are called viruses. These can range from harmless but irritating programs (for example, a message springing up on your monitor every five minutes saying 'Happy Birthday!') to programs that could disable your computer.

Anti-virus programs constantly scan your PC for the viruses and delete them before any damage is done. Anti-virus software should be installed as soon as the computer is set up and running. Most new PCs come with anti-virus software; check before you buy.

A second type of unwanted program is spyware, which logs the keystrokes you make as you type on your computer and sends the information to the hacker who can use it to work out information about you, such as your passwords. To protect yourself from this kind of attack, install a good anti-spyware program, which scans your computer for these programs and deletes them.

With a good firewall and anti-virus software, the possibility of a hacker managing to disable your computer is slim. If the worst did happen, however, your computer helpline service should talk you through bringing your computer back to life.

Backing up your work

It is a good idea to keep a back-up copy of your files just in case anything goes wrong with the computer. You can do this in a variety of ways, listed below, such as floppy disks, USB sticks and CDs. Store these separately from your PC.

If anything does go wrong and you have to start from scratch, you will have not have lost any of your documents.

Removable storage

Apart from using them for back-up, copying information on to a portable disk means you can move documents from one PC to another. If someone e-mails you some photographs, for example, you may want to take them to the photo shop to be printed out professionally.

None of these options will store as much as your computer, so the amount they will hold is always measured in Megabytes (MB) not Gigabytes. Some can store more information than others.

Each type of disk is inserted into its own special slots on the computer called a 'drive'.

Floppy disk

Also called a floppy, this looks like a small square of hard plastic: the 'floppy' is the magnetic disk hidden inside. One disk does not hold much information (only about 1.44 MB) so it is only useful for smaller text documents. You can use a floppy disk as many times as you like by simply 'throwing away' what's on it when you have finished with it, and copying something else. Some PCs no longer have floppy disk drives because people are now using other options.

Source: ImagExtra (www.andyjonesdesign.co.uk/imagextra)

USB sticks

Also called USB keys, USB sticks are tiny storage devices about the size of a flattened AA battery. They hold more than 10 or even 100 times more information than a floppy (they vary in size from about 64MB to 2GB) so they can be used for almost anything. You can use them as many times as you like by simply throwing away what's on them when you have finished with it, and copying something else. There are USB1 and USB2 media sticks. A USB2 media stick can be used in a USB1 or USB2 connection.

Courtesy: pixmania.co.uk

CD

Short for Compact Disk, CDs are the familiar round silver disks. These can store up to 700MB of data. To save documents on to a CD, your PC must have a CD writer, sometimes called a burner; most new computers will have this. Most CDs can be written to only once; some can be used over and over again.

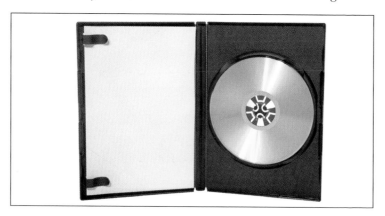

DVD

Short for Digital Versatile Disk, a DVD looks just the same as a CD. These disks have masses of space and can hold a minimum of around 5GB of data, which is enough to store a full-length movie. As with CDs, DVD drives come in two types – one that can only read data from a DVD and a second that can both read and write data on to the disk.

Use your common sense while surfing

You wouldn't walk down an unlit street on your own at midnight down the wrong end of town, so just use a similar level of common sense on the internet.

- Only allow people you know to use your PC.

- Choose a reputable internet service provider.

- Use passwords that you can remember but are not too obvious. The most common password is 'password'!

- No reputable person will ever e-mail you asking for personal details in an open e-mail.

- When making any online transactions, stick to companies with a recognisable and reputable presence outside the internet.

- Be careful about giving away personal details unless it is absolutely necessary, and then only when you are sure whom you are giving them to. If you are putting in personal or financial details, the site will tell you that you are on a 'secure' page.

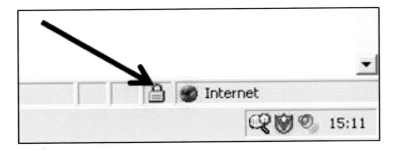

- Whenever a credit card transaction is called for, make sure you can see a small padlock icon on the bottom right-hand corner of your computer screen. This is an indication that any data exchanged between your PC and the online site is encrypted and is therefore confidential.

- If you are not happy about something, just leave the site. You can change your mind at any stage of a transaction until you press the final 'Confirm' button.

But don't let this worry you because most surfing is anonymous and fun so you only need have your guard up when you are dealing with personal or financial information. Most people on the net are there to help you and give you a good service, so do enjoy yourself!

Your reminder box

- A firewall prevents unauthorised access to your computer.

- An anti-virus program prevents rogue programs getting into your computer.

- Make copies of your work just in case anything goes wrong.

- You can store information on a removable floppy disk, a media stick, a CD or a DVD.

- Use your common sense while surfing: don't give away personal information.

Chapter 4
E-mails

This is where we actually get down to business and in the next half an hour, you will be able to send an e-mail. It is so easy, you'll get the hang of it in no time.

E-mail just stands for electronic mail, which makes it the internet equivalent of letter-writing but without the stationery and stamps and waiting for days for mail to arrive! E-mails can be sent to and received from anywhere in the world and take only seconds to arrive at their destination, regardless of where in the world that is. It is easy to understand how e-mail works because it is a lot like a normal postal service, only your e-mail is delivered to a virtual post-box provided by your ISP.

All you need to send and receive e-mail is:

- an e-mail program to read and send e-mail – the most common program is Outlook Express, usually just called Outlook, which will be on your computer when you buy it;

- an internet connection to an ISP – which you have just set up;

- an e-mail address – which your ISP will give you.

Your e-mail address will look something like this:

hbrookes@myisp.com

Notice how the e-mail address is made up of characters separated by an @ sign (pronounced 'at'). The first half of the e-mail address is made up of any combination of letters and numbers you choose, and can be your real name if you like. The second half is usually the ISP's name.

The difference between e-mails and web addresses

- An e-mail address is your virtual post box. It includes your name, an @ and your ISP's name.

- A web address is the address of a web site or web page and usually starts with www.

What you see when you open the program

Find the Outlook Express icon on your desktop and double-click it. The program starts and you see something like this:

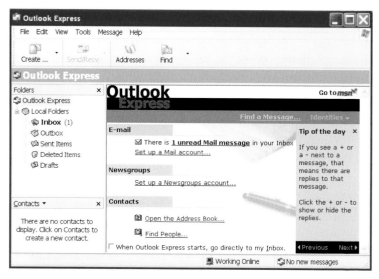

Don't be put off. We'll look at it a bit at a time and you'll soon feel quite at home.

The Menu Bar

The bars across the top are called Toolbars. At the top is the Menu Bar with various buttons to help you do various tasks when you are working on your e-mails.

Simply clicking on an item listed on the Menu Bar reveals a list of options. You will learn how to use these as we go along when you need to get something done.

Toolbar

Underneath the Menu Bar is the Toolbar. Initially, you only see four buttons for your most common tasks.

- a **Create** button for quickly creating new e-mails;

- a **Send/Receive** button to send and fetch mail from the internet;

- an **Address** button for your Address Book;

- a **Find** button for searching for specific e-mails or address book entries.

Later on, depending on what task you are performing, more buttons, with little icons indicating what they do, may appear. Once you've learnt what the little icons mean, it will become second nature to click on them to perform various tasks, such as printing an e-mail, with a single click of the mouse.

The main window

When you open Outlook Express for the very first time, you will see a window divided into three panes. Down the right-hand side are two panes, a **Folders** pane, which neatly groups together different types of e-mails, and a **Contacts** pane, where your Address Book entries will go. The larger pane on the left has some links for **E-mail**, **Newsgroups** and **Contacts**. You will learn how to use these in a moment.

Take a second look at the **Folders** pane. The **Inbox** folder holds all the e-mails you receive. The total number of unread e-mails is always shown in brackets so you don't miss any new messages. Click once now on the word **Inbox** in the **Folders** pane. The view in the right-hand pane changes to reveal two new panes. The top one holds the list of received e-mails, while the bottom half is a **Preview** pane that allows you to view a message quickly without opening a separate window. For now, there is just one e-mail, a welcome message from Microsoft Outlook.

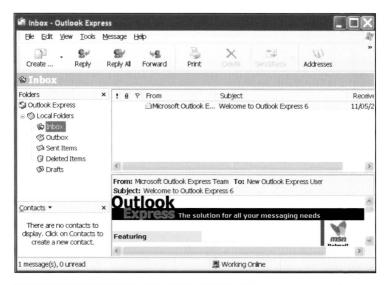

The Scroll Bar

Down the right-hand side of the Preview window is a Scroll Bar. Scroll Bars appear on a program window whenever the window has more content than can be displayed at one time. To use the Scroll Bar, just point to it with your mouse, click once and, without letting go, move the pointer downwards. This is called clicking and dragging and allows you to see the rest of the content of a window or pane.

Don't worry **about the mouse scroll button**

Once you are happy using your mouse, you may want to use the scroller in the middle. Click on a window and rotate the button (as though you were stroking the mouse's head!) and you will scroll quickly down the page.

Setting up your e-mail program

A mail server is simply a computer that manages all your e-mail going to and from your computer; this is run by your ISP. When you sign up with an ISP, they will give you step-by-step instructions to connect to their system. Once this connection has been set up correctly, your computer will be able to send and receive e-mails.

Setting up your e-mail program manually

If your ISP does not provide the step-by-step guidance, don't worry. This is what you do.

You will need:

- **Program:** an e-mail program such as Outlook, which will already be on your computer.

- **Account information:** your name as you would like it to appear to others when they receive e-mail from you; your e-mail-address people should use when sending you e-mail.

- **Logon information:** your Username that identifies your e-mail account; your password to access your account.

- **Server information:** incoming mail server and outgoing mail server, which are the names of the computers at your ISP that send mail in and out.

Step 1 From the **Tools** menu, find and click once on **Accounts**. The **Internet Accounts** window opens. Notice the four tabs headed **All**, **Mail**, **News** and **Directory Service**. Make sure the **Mail** tab is selected. Ignore the others for now.

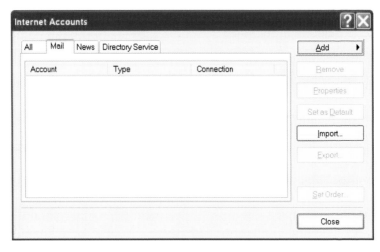

Step 2 Click once on the **Add** button on the top left corner. On the menu that appears, click once on the **Mail** option. The **Internet Connection** wizard for e-mail starts and the **Your Name** window appears.

Step 3 Type in your name as you would like it to appear to someone receiving your e-mail and click **Next**. The **Internet E-mail Address** window appears.

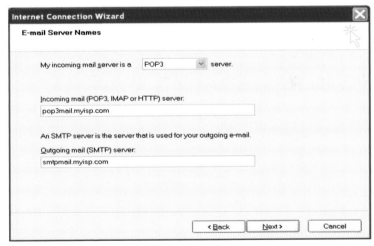

Step 4 Type in your e-mail address and click **Next**. The **E-mail Server Names** window appears.

Step 5 Click once on the little down-arrow at the end of the box labelled 'My incoming mail server is a' and select the appropriate server type (POP3, IMAP or HTTP), as detailed by your ISP. In the other two boxes, fill in the names for your incoming and outgoing mail servers given to you by your IPS and click **Next**. The Internet Mail Logon window appears.

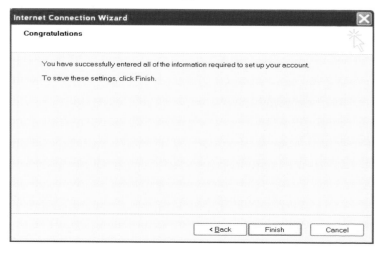

Step 6 Once again, fill in the account name and password given to you by your ISP. Unless you've been advised otherwise, leave empty the box labelled **Log on using Secure Password Authentication (SPA)** and click **Next**. The final window appears. Click once on the **Finish** button. The wizard closes and you are taken back to the **Internet Accounts** window, where your new e-mail account is now listed.

Free e-mail

You can also use an online e-mail service, which allows you to receive and send e-mail from any PC connected to the internet. Examples are Yahoo!'s free online e-mail service, or MSN's hotmail.

How to receive an e-mail

Now the fun begins! First you have to get someone to send you an e-mail! Give all your friends your e-mail address and wait for your mail to start arriving.

Step 1 Log on to the internet.

Step 2 Open Outlook Express by double-clicking on the icon on the desktop. Outlook automatically fetches new e-mail from the internet. If this does not happen, you can fetch e-mail by clicking once on the **Send/Receive** button on the Toolbar.

Step 3 You will see a list of your new e-mails in your Inbox.

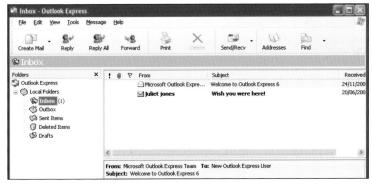

Step 4 To read an e-mail, simply double-click it. The e-mail will open in a new separate window.

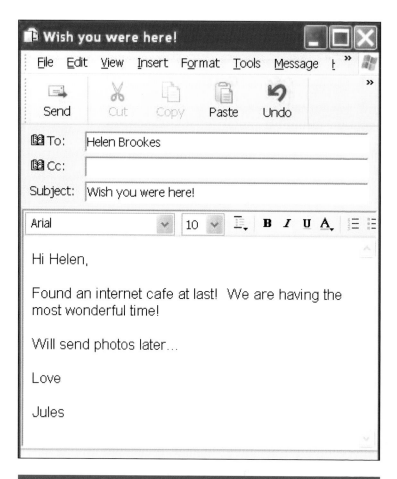

How to reply

This is equally easy!

Step 1 You have your e-mail open. Click once on the **Reply** button on the Toolbar.

Step 2 A new window opens up with a blank page ready for you to type in your reply. The original message you received is repeated at the bottom of the page. All you need to do is type your reply in the space above it.

Everything else is already filled in.

Step 3 When you've finished, click once on the **Send** button, also found on the Toolbar, and that's it!

If you are connected to the internet, Outlook will automatically send the e-mail. If not, just click once on the **Send/Receive** button on the Toolbar to connect to the mail server so that the e-mail is sent.

How to write and send an e-mail

Sending your own e-mails is just as simple and you follow a similar procedure so you should now be confident about what to do.

Step 1 To write a new e-mail, click once on the **Create** button on the Toolbar. A new window opens up.

Step 2 In the **To** box, type in the e-mail address of the person you want to write to.

Step 3 In the **Subject** box, type in a short heading for your e-mail.

Step 4 Now, in the main window, type in your e-mail message.

Step 5 Press **Send/Receive**, as you did before – and off it goes.

Sending to several people at once

If you want to send the same e-mail to more than one person, type in the e-mail address of the first person in the **To** box, then type in a semi-colon after it.

Now type in the next person's e-mail address – and keep adding as many as you like.

You can also use the **CC** box (short for carbon copy) to send a copy of the e-mail to someone else. Just type their e-mail address in the box.

If you want to send a copy of an e-mail to someone without the main recipient knowing, type his or her name in the **BCC** (blind carbon copy) box.

Filling in your address book

To save having to type in e-mail addresses every time you want to send an e-mail, you can make yourself an address book. Once an address is in the book, you can simply type the person's name in the In box when you want to send them an e-mail, and the computer will remember the address for you.

Here's how you do it.

Step 1 Open Outlook Express.

Step 2 Click on **Addresses** at the top.

Step 3 Click on **New** and a menu will drop down.

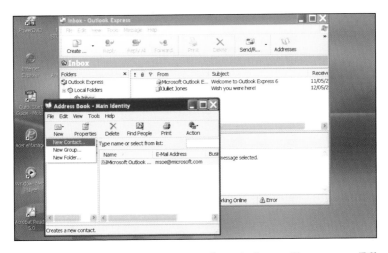

Step 4 Click on **New contact** and a window will open up. Fill in the boxes with the name and e-mail of the person. You don't have to fill them all in.

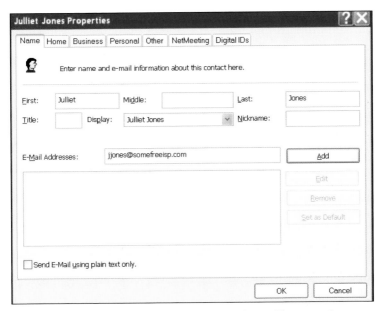

Step 5 Click on **Add**, then **OK** – and you'll never have to remember that e-mail address again!

Now try it out by sending them an e-mail. Click on **Create** to open a new e-mail. Start to type in the person's name and their name and e-mail will appear so you can stop typing and press **Enter**.

You can add as many people to your address book as you want, and as much detail on each one as you need.

Attachments

Sometimes you will receive an e-mail with a little paper-clip symbol next to it in the Inbox. That means someone has sent you an attachment – a picture or a document as well as the e-mail itself, just as you might attach a photo to a letter before you send it.

How to look at an attachment

Step 1 Open the e-mail just as you would normally.
Step 2 Double-click on the attachment name or icon. A small window appears asking whether you wish to open the file. Click once on **Open** and it will open up.

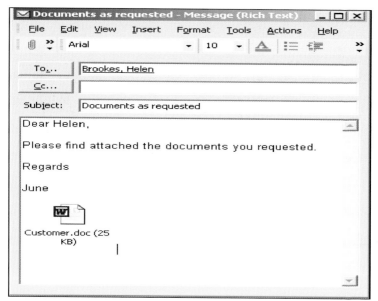

Don't worry **about spam**

The internet equivalent of junk mail, spam is unsolicited e-mail sent from sources other than your known contacts and is often used as a marketing tool. At best spam is irritating, at worst dangerous since it can contain viruses.

Don't open it. Don't read it – and certainly don't reply to it.

The best thing to do with spam is simply delete it.

Step 1 Single-click on the e-mail in your Inbox.

Step 2 Press **Delete** on the Toolbar to send the e-mail to **Deleted Items**.

Step 3 Double-click on **Deleted Items** on the left-hand side of the screen.

Step 4 Single-click on the e-mail, then press **Delete**. You may be asked if you are sure you want to delete the item. Just click on Yes.

You can delete any other e-mails in the same way.

You can set up Outlook to filter persistent spammers. Click once on the unwanted message to highlight it, then click on the **Message** menu at the top of the screen. Find the **Block Sender** option and click on it once. You can unblock an e-mail address from the **Block Senders** list found under the **Message Rules** options on the **Tools** menu.

See page 93 for more about spam.

How to send an attachment

If you want to send a photograph, or another document, with your e-mails, you can do the same using the **Attach** button on the Toolbar. This is the one that looks like a paper-clip.

To try this out, you need to decide on a photo you would like to send someone. Make a note of its name and save it on the computer in the folder My Documents.

Step 1 Create a new e-mail and type in your message as usual.

Step 2 Click once on the **Attachment** button on the Toolbar. The **Insert Attachment** window opens.

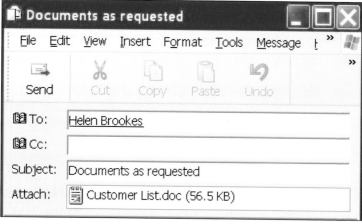

Step 3 Now you need to find the picture. Click on the bar at the top and a menu will open up. Move your cursor to **My Documents** and click so the window fills with a list of your documents.

Step 4 Find the document you want and double-click. The attachment will appear as an icon labelled with the name of the file. Click **Send** to send your e-mail together with the attachment.

Problems with attachments

If you cannot open an attachment, it usually means that your PC does not have the program that was used to create it. You can remedy this by installing the relevant program or asking the sender to send a new attachment created in software you already have on your computer.

Be careful

You have to be careful with attachments because they are sometimes used by hackers to send viruses that could damage your PC. Never open an attachment sent from an e-mail address you do not recognise. Just delete the e-mail.

Making the text look good

Once you have practised sending and receiving some e-mails, you may want to play around with the look of your e-mails. You can change what the text looks like – the font – what size it appears, and so on.

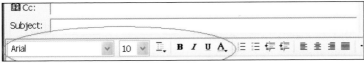

How to change the text font

Step 1 Look on the Toolbar at the box labelled 'Arial'. Click once on the arrow and hold your finger on the mouse button and a menu will drop down.

Step 2 Slide your cursor down the list, then click once with your mouse to select a font you like. The e-mail will then be written in that font.

How to change the text size

Find the little box on the menu bar with '10' in it. Do exactly as you did with the font: click the arrow, slide the cursor to the size you want and click on it to select it.

How to change the text colour

Step 1　Type some text into your e-mail. Click to the left of the text, then drag the cursor over the text to highlight it. Let go of the mouse button.

Step 2　Find the letter 'A' button with the colour beneath it. Click on the arrow, drag your cursor to the colour you want and click on it once to select it. Click anywhere away from the box to unhighlight it and reveal the new colour.

How to change the text style

Highlight the text you want to change, as above. Then click on the **B**, *I* or U buttons to change it to **bold**, *italic* or underline.

When you've finished, click once on the **Send** button on the Toolbar to send your e-mail.

Security note

Do not send sensitive information (bank details, etc.) by e-mail as they can be intercepted.

You may receive an e-mail that contains a link to a website. This will look like an underlined web address and when you move your cursor over it, the cursor will turn into a hand. Click once, and it will take you straight to the website.

If this is a website you want to visit, it's a really useful device. But don't use any such link from a spam e-mail or one from a source you don't recognise.

Your reminder box

- Double-click on an e-mail in your **Inbox** to open it.

- Click on **Reply** to send a reply.

- Click on **Create** to send a new e-mail.

- Click on **Send/Receive** to send and receive e-mails.

- Click on **Attach** to add an attachment.

- Use the text editing buttons to change the text.

- Do not open e-mail attachments from a source you do not recognise.

- Do not open or reply to spam – simply delete it.

- Change the look of your e-mail by varying the font style.

Chapter 5
Let's Go Surfing

Your computer is all set up, your connection to the internet works and you are raring to go! In this chapter you'll learn all the basics about finding your way around the web without getting lost. We'll do everything one step at a time and we'll just tell you what you need to know to get going.

Getting on the net

Your computer will already have a program called a browser. A browser is simply a computer program that fetches and displays internet web pages. To get on the net, you need to open your browser program.

The two best-known browsers are Microsoft's Internet Explorer and Netscape Navigator. They both work in exactly the same way so it doesn't matter which one is on your computer.

Don't worry **about minor differences**

Because the computer programmers are constantly updating everything, you might see something slightly different from the illustrations shown here or from one computer to another. It makes no difference to what you are doing.

Here is what you do.

Step 1 Switch on your computer and wait until you can see the screen and various items on it. This is your desktop.

Step 2 Double-click on the icon you created in Chapter 2 to connect you to your ISP, then on **Dial** when the next window opens.

Step 3 At the bottom left-hand corner, you'll see the **Start** button. Click on it once and a menu will pop up.

Step 4 Move your cursor to the words **All Programs** and click once. Another menu will pop up.

Step 5 Find **Internet Explorer** on the list and click on it once.

Step 6 If you're using Netscape Navigator, find the word **Netscape**, click on it once and a second menu appears. Click once on **Navigator**.

The computer will open up the program. That's it!

Quick method of starting the browser

Find the browser icon on your desktop. It should look something like this:

Double-click it to start the browser.

What you'll see

The browser opens a new window with a web page on it. What you see on your screen depends on your browser program and who you are using to connect you to the internet (your ISP).

This shows what you will see if you open in Internet Explorer.

This shows what you will see if you open in Netscape Navigator.

This first page you see is called your **home page**, because it is the first web page you see every time you start surfing. Later on, you will learn how to change your home page to one of your choice (see page 75).

At first glance there seems to be a lot going on, so we'll do a quick tour round the page so you feel comfortable with what you are looking at. Then we'll explain each bit only when you need to use it to get something done.

The Menu Bar

The bars across the top are called Toolbars. At the top is the Menu Bar with various buttons to help you do various tasks when you are surfing.

Simply clicking on an item listed on the Menu Bar reveals a list of options. You will learn how to use these as we go along when you need to get something done.

Standard Buttons Bar

Underneath the Menu Bar is the Standard Buttons Bar. Once you've learnt what the little icons mean, it will become second nature to click on them to perform various tasks, such as printing a web page, with a single click of the mouse.

The Address Bar

Underneath that is the Address Bar. This is called the Navigation Bar in Netscape.

The Scroll Bar

Down the right-hand side of the window is the Scroll Bar. This appears whenever the web page has more content than you can see on your screen. Click on it and drag downwards with your mouse to see the rest of the page (or just hit the **Page Down** key on your keyboard).

How to get somewhere

That's all you need to know to make a start. For the rest of this chapter, we'll show you how to get things done, and you'll learn about the buttons and bars as you go along.

Just like a house, every website has an address that takes you straight to it. The address – not surprisingly! – appears in the Address Bar. A complete web address looks something like this:

http://www.foulsham.com

Ignore the http:// bit – you don't need it.

Don't worry **about web address endings**

At the end of a web address, you are most likely to see .com but you might see .co.uk – which means it's a UK site – or .de – which means it's German – and so on. Other sites might end in .org or .net or something else entirely.

After the .com, you might see a forward slash / and some text. That just sends you to a different part of the site.

Surfing is the term we learnt right at the beginning for when you visit different websites. The easiest way to do this is to simply type in the website address on to the Address Bar. Have a go right now.

Click your mouse in the Address Bar and highlight the home page address you can see there. Type in the following web address:

www.tesco.com

Then click once on the **Go** button at the right-hand end of the Address Bar or press once on the Enter [⏎] key of your keypad. The Tesco home page will appear in the window.

Now you can go anywhere you like – all you need is the address! Web addresses can be found everywhere: on advertisements, business cards, TV, literally anywhere. You can also find them on the web itself and in a minute you'll learn how.

Pop-ups

Pop-ups are small windows containing advertisements that appear (unrequested) on your screen. You can simply close them by clicking on the box in the top right-hand corner. There are programs that will block them if you want to follow that up later on.

How to get back

On the left-hand end of the Standard Buttons toolbar are the **Back** and **Forward** buttons. These allow you to move back and forth between web pages you have recently visited.

To go back to your home page, click once on the **Back** button. The Tesco site is replaced by your original one.

Now click on the **Forward** button and you'll go to Tesco again.

As we've already learnt, web addresses can be found in lots of places. Practise surfing by typing in the addresses you find on the advertisements and visiting their sites. Type the addresses in the Address Bar. Use your own, or try the following:

www.foulsham.com

www.amazon.co.uk

www.thehungersite.com

www.bbc.co.uk

www.saga.co.uk

www.seniorsnetwork.co.uk

You have now visited enough sites to do a bit of navigating! Take a moment to experiment with the **Back** and **Forward** buttons to see how you can quickly retrieve web pages that you recently visited.

Don't worry **if the address changes**

Don't worry if you type in an address in the Address Bar and it changes once it has taken you to the site. It makes no difference to you.

What if you make a mistake?

It really doesn't matter!

If the browser recognises the address you have keyed in, it will take you there – even if it's not where you wanted to be – just as the postman will deliver a letter to number 16 if that's what you wrote on the envelope even though your friend lives at number 6. Just check the address and key it in again.

If the browser doesn't recognise the address, it can't take you there. A window will pop up saying:

The specified server could not be found.

Just click the OK button, check what you typed and key it in again. Try keying in:

ww.tesco.co.uk

and you'll see what happens.

Don't worry **if you key in the wrong address**

Sometimes when you key in a wrong address, you may find a site pops up offering to sell you the address or offering other links. If it's not what you want, just ignore it.

Moving around a website

Most websites have more than one page and will have links that take you to the next page. If you move your mouse over a link, the arrow will turn into a hand. Click on the link once and you will automatically be taken to that page.

Getting some practice

You should now be able to do a bit of surfing on your own. Look around you and find any newspapers, leaflets and other items with web addresses on them and use your new-found skills to view them on the internet. Use the **Back** and **Forward** buttons, **Home** button and **Favorites** or **Bookmarked** links to navigate between different pages and sites. Feel free to repeat any exercises until you feel completely comfortable working with your browser.

Your reminder box

- Go online by double-clicking on **Connect to the Internet** on your desktop.

- **Start, Programs, Internet Explorer** will open your internet program.

- Type a web address in the **Address Bar** and press **Go** to take you to a website.

- The **Back** and **Forward** buttons help you move from one site to another.

- The **Scroll Bar** at the side helps you move up and down the page.

- The links help you move around the pages in a website.

Chapter 6

Gaining Confidence

In this chapter, we are going to look at a few more simple tasks for getting used to surfing and setting up your computer how you want it.

How to print a web page

This is very easily done because you have a **Print** button on the Internet Explorer's Standard Buttons Bar at the top of the screen ...

... or, on the top right-hand corner on the Netscape Navigator window.

All you need to do is click once on the button. The current web page is immediately sent to the printer for printing.

How to set your home page

As we mentioned earlier, your home page is the one that automatically opens up first so it makes sense to make it one of your choice, rather than the default one that comes with your internet service provider. It is easy to do. For now, we will set your home page to the Yahoo! UK home page, which we are going to use again for the next job. This is done using the Menu Bar options.

Setting your home page with Internet Explorer

Step 1 Click once on **Tools** on the Menu Bar and a menu will drop down.

Step 2 Click once on **Internet Options** and a window will open.

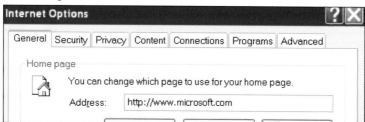

Step 3 You will see that there are a number of tabs across the top and that the **General** tab is currently being shown. Underneath that is the **Address** field, which shows the address of your current home page.

Step 4 Click once in the **Address** field box. Press **Delete** until the current home page address has disappeared, then type in the following web address instead:

www.yahoo.co.uk

Step 5 Click once on **OK** to complete the exercise. Your home page has now been set to **www.yahoo.co.uk**. The next time you start your browser, you will be sent directly to the Yahoo! UK site.

To test your new setting, click once of the **Home** button on the Standard Buttons Bar. You are immediately taken to the Yahoo! UK site which is now your new home page.

If you like the page you are on

If you are online and you want to choose the page you are at as your home page, follow steps 1 and 2, then click on **Use Current**, then click on **OK**.

Setting your home page with Netscape Navigator

Step 1 Click once on **Edit** on the Menu Bar and a menu will pop up.

Step 2 Click once on **Preferences** and another menu will appear.

Step 3 Look at the list on the left-hand side. Click once on **Navigator** and the right-hand side of the page will change.

Step 4 Find the box labelled **Location** half way down the page. Delete the current home page address and replace with the following web address:

www.yahoo.co.uk

Step 5 Click once on **OK** to complete the exercise. Your home page has now been set to **www.yahoo.co.uk**. The next time you start your browser, you will be sent directly to the Yahoo! UK site.

How to check your home page

To test your new setting, click once on the **Home** button found just beneath the **Back** and **Forward** buttons on the Menu Bar. You are immediately taken to the Yahoo! UK site, which is your new your home page.

How to make the words bigger

Most computers display sites with medium-sized text. If you find the text on your screen is too small, just change it! You can make it smaller or larger as you prefer.

To change the text size using Internet Explorer

Step 1 Click once on **View** on the Menu Bar and a menu will drop down.

Step 2 Click once on **Text Size** and a second menu appears giving you a choice of five text sizes.

Step 3 Click once on **Largest** and watch how the size of text on the screen changes.

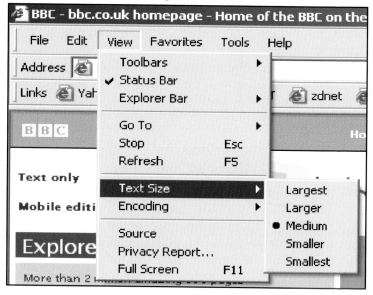

You can repeat this exercise with other text size options until you find one that suits you.

To change the text size using Netscape Navigator

This exercise is even simpler if you are using Netscape Navigator because you just use the keyboard.

Step 1 Find the **CTRL** (Control) key on the bottom left-hand corner or your keyboard and the plus (+) and minus (−) signs on the number pad.

Step 2 To increase the text size, hold down **CTRL** and hit the **PLUS** key a few times. Watch how the text on the screen gets larger.

Step 3 To decrease the text size, hold down **CTRL** and hit the **MINUS** key a few times. The text size gets smaller.

How to find your favourites easily

As you begin to surf, you'll find sites that you will want to go back to on a regular basis. To save you having to type the web address on to the Address Bar each time you want to go there, you can save them in your **Favorites** (note the American spelling).

Don't worry **about bookmarking!**

If someone talks to you about 'bookmarking', it's just a short-hand way of saying you've listed sites in your favourites.

eBay is one of the world's most recognised online auction sites. We are going to use that as an example to show you how to put it in your Favorites.

Saving a favourite site using Internet Explorer

Step 1 Go to the eBay home page by typing **www.ebay.co.uk** in the **Address Bar** and clicking on **Go** or pressing **Enter**.

Step 2 Click once on **Favorites** on the Menu Bar at the top and a menu will drop down.

Step 3 Click once on **Add to Favorites** and a window appears with the name 'eBay UK – the UK's Online marketplace' in the Name box.

Step 4 Click **OK** and that's it!

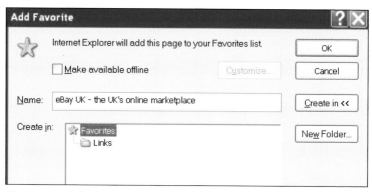

To test your link, go back to your home page by clicking once on the **Home** button on the Standard Buttons Bar. Click once on **Favorites** and a list will open at the side of the screen. Click once on the eBay listing and it will take you straight there. To close the Favorites window, click once on Favorites again.

Saving a favourite site using Netscape Navigator

Step 1 Go to the eBay home page by typing **www.ebay.co.uk** in the **Address Bar** and clicking on **Go** or pressing **Enter**.

Step 2 Click once on **Bookmarks** and a menu will appear.

Step 3 Click once on **Bookmark This Page**. A link to the eBay UK home page is immediately added to the Bookmarks list and the menu disappears. That's it!

To test your link, go back to your home page by clicking once on the **Home** button just beneath the **Back** and **Forward** buttons. Click once on **Bookmarks**. Then click on the new link listed.

Now there's no stopping you

Now you have all the skills you need to start doing a bit of surfing on your own. Look around you and find any newspapers, leaflets and other items with web addresses on them and use your new-found skills to view them on the internet. Play around with the **Back** and **Forward** buttons, the **Home** button and **Favorites** links to navigate your way around. Once you have a bit of practice, you'll soon feel comfortable with all these processes and you'll be eager to learn some more skills.

Your reminder box

- Use **Home** to go straight to your home page.

- Use the **Scroll bar** to move up and down a web page.

- Visit any site by typing the web address in the **Address Bar**.

- Use the **Back** and **Forward** buttons to move between sites.

- Use **Print** to print a page.

- Use **View**, **Text Size** to make the text bigger or smaller.

- Change the home page by clicking on **Tools**, then **Internet Options**.

- Set sites as favourites by visiting the site, then clicking on **Favorites**, then **Add to Favorites**.

- Open and close the Favorites window by clicking on **Favorites**.

Chapter 7

How To Find What You Want

You have already found many sources of addresses for websites you might want to visit, but there are millions more out there waiting to be discovered!

If you'd like to visit a particular website but do not know what its web address is, you can use what's called a search engine. Or if you want to find out about a particular topic and you don't know where to go – holidays in Tunisia, for example – you can use the search engine to show you what's available.

Search engines work by finding websites that contain a certain word or phrase. You choose the word or words you want to search for, type them in and press the button. The search results are given to you in the form of a list that has links to the websites it finds. You simply click on the link that looks like the one you want.

We'll show you how they work using two of the most popular search engines: Yahoo! and Google.

Try a simple task

Here's a simple task to show you how it works; let's find a last-minute holiday on Yahoo!

Step 1 You have already set Yahoo! UK as your home page, so to get there you can simply press the **Home** button or type the following address on to the **Address Bar**:

www.yahoo.co.uk

The Yahoo! UK home page appears.

Step 2 You will see a space that allows you to type in your search words, and beside it, a large **Search** button. The words you use to search are called keywords.

Step 3 Type the words **last minute travel** in the box and click once on **Search**. You get a list of all sites that contain your search words, with links to those websites:

Step 4 The first item listed looks like a sure guess. Click once on it. The Lastminute.com home page appears.

Step 5 If that's not what you wanted, use your **Back** button to go back to the search list and try another link. You can do that as often as you like until you find a site that gives you the information you need.

Finding your way around Google

Another very well-known search engine is Google, found at **www.google.com**. Type the address in the **Address Bar** and take a look. You might want to add it to your favourites, or make it your home page.

In the middle of the screen, you'll see the space to type in your keywords with two buttons underneath it. Try an example. Type in:

Oxford University

and press **Google Search** to start the search.

In a few seconds, a list of websites will appear on the screen. They will be listed in order according to their relevance to your search with those considered most relevant placed at the top of the list. Its ability to rank search results in this way is one reason why Google has become such a popular search engine. In this case, the first one will be

www.ox.ac.uk

which is the one you want. Move your cursor to the name and it will turn into a hand, which, as you know, means it's a link. Click on the link and it will take you to the Oxford University website.

Don't forget Enter

Hitting the **Enter** key on your keyboard has the same effect as clicking on **Google Search**.

Now go back to Google and again type in:

Oxford University

but this time click on **I'm feeling Lucky**. This time, Google will take you straight to the very first web page that most closely matches your query, so you go straight to Oxford University's home page.

How to target your search

How to choose the right keywords

Choosing different keywords will make a big difference to the results you get, so think about what you type in. The more precise you can be, the more likely you are to find what you want.

Avoid words that apply to too many things. For example:

- 'advice' could take you almost anywhere;
- 'health advice' would only offer you about half as many options;
- 'health advice arthritis' will cut down the numbers to just three per cent of that so it will be much more effective in taking you where you want to go (and you'll still have three million choices!);
- 'health advice older people' will cut it down again.

Google will ignore small words like 'and' and 'with' so leave them out.

How to search UK sites

Look again at the Google home page underneath the Search buttons. You'll see two more options: **Search the web** and **Search pages from the UK**.

Narrow down your search by clicking on the UK button.

Incidentally, if you are looking for pictures rather than words, you can use Google's image search function. To do this, click on **Images**, above the bar where you would type the keywords for your search. In the new page that opens, type in the keywords for your search, then click on **Image Search** and you will be taken to a page or results of pictures. If you're feeling confident, you can refine your search even further by selecting **Advanced Image Search**, which will allow you to find pictures of a specific size and, for those who know about such things, format.

How to use phrases

So far, your results returned documents that listed the keywords in any order or combination. You can also use quotes around a phrase in a search engine to make sure you only get documents and web pages including that exact phrase. For example, if you search for:

health advice older people uk

you'll get this result:

But if you search for:

'health advice' 'older people' uk

you'll get this result:

Now you can try all sorts of search experiments for yourself so you really get the hang of it. Remember: it really doesn't matter if you go to a site by mistake, or you find the site you visit is not what you thought it would be. Just press your **Back** button to go back to the previous page, or press **Home** to go back to your home page at any time.

Your reminder box

- Find new sites using a search engine.

- Two popular search engines are **www.yahoo.co.uk** and **www.google.co.uk**.

- Type in the keywords you are looking for and click on **Search** or press **Enter**.

- If you click on **I'm feeling lucky**, it will take you direct to the most appropriate site.

- Use specific words to narrow your search.

- Visit any sites listed by clicking on the name.

- Put quotes around groups of words so they are treated as one phrase.

Chapter 8

Let's Go Shopping

Buying things over the internet has several advantages over going to the shop, the most obvious one being convenience. All you do is place your order on the appropriate website and voila! it all arrives in the post. No more fighting crowds in the rain. No more worrying about opening times. You can shop whenever you feel like it, even if it's in the dead of night!

The second reason that shopping over the internet has become so popular is the savings that can be made online. On average, items bought over the internet tend to be cheaper that shop-bought items, even when you include postage and delivery costs. When doing bulk shopping such as for Christmas gifts, the savings can be considerable.

Am I likely to have problems?

This may be the first question you ask, so let's start with some reassurance. Things can go wrong with internet shopping, just as they can with any mail-order or high-street purchase, but most people shop on the internet with perfect ease and safety.

Most bad experiences with internet shopping arise from online shoppers not applying the same discretion to vendors as one might a high-street store. Most people would not buy a fridge freezer from a van at a street corner, but fail to use the same judgement over the internet. Because anyone can open an online store, it is important to vet online vendors in the same way you would 'real life' traders.

- Try to stick with companies that have a reputable presence outside the internet.

- Make sure they offer secure, encrypted online purchasing.

- Always research anyone else fully. Do they have a physical (not mailbox) address? Do they have a reachable telephone number? Is the company registered? Are you using them on the recommendation of someone who's had a good experience with them? Do not continue until you are completely satisfied with the answers to these questions.

- If in doubt, don't buy.

Registering at a site as a member

Some websites require you to register as a member before being able to browse or shop online. Registration is almost always free. In most cases all you need to do is supply your e-mail address. In turn, you are given a username and password that allow you to log on to the site, giving you access to pages not available to unregistered users.

- Keep the same username for all the sites you register at to make it easy to remember.

- You can also use the same password but remember the safety points outlined on page 45.

Sometimes registration will involve filling in personal information, such as your postal address, and in some cases (for example, where an online service is being offered), registration could involve a fee.

Obviously, if you make a purchase, you'll need to fill in delivery and payment information.

Why do they need my details?

Site owners use the information supplied by registered users in different ways. Most use your e-mail to create a mailing list so they can occasionally e-mail you with special offers or other advertising material.

If you don't want to receive them:

- Go online.

- Open the e-mail.

- Scroll down to the bottom of the e-mail and find **Unsubscribe**.

- Click on the link.

It may take you straight to their site where you will confirm that you don't want to receive any more e-mails. It may open a new e-mail so you can send them an e-mail confirming you don't want to hear from them again.

However, like with your postal address, giving away your e-mail address could mean you ending up with junk mail. Less scrupulous website owners have been known to sell their mailing lists to people called spammers, who send out such junk mail (see page 61). The best way to avoid this is simply to register only with reputable sites.

Don't worry **about spam**

If you only give your e-mail address to reputable people, you should not receive junk e-mail, called spam. However, you could set up a separate e-mail address just for registering on websites. If it does get sold to spammers, you could just abandon it.

If you want to do this, go to **www.hotmail.com** and follow the instructions.

How to shop

Start by choosing your online shop and make sure you are happy to do business with them. Visit their home page and have a look round. Remember, there are several ways you can find a business's web address, such as looking at any advertising or marketing material, or by using a search engine.

In this exercise we will use Tesco's online shopping site.

Type:

www.tesco.com

into your Address Bar to bring up its online shopping website.

Notice how Tesco has divided its home page into different sections. The main page lists several different Category links such as Groceries, Finance, etc. There is also some advertising on the right-hand side. Across the top of the page are **Tabs**, each of which is link to a different web page on the site.

Notice the icons on the top right-hand corner. Most online shopping sites will have similar ones.

- A **shopping basket** is a page that will contain a list of items you have selected to buy.

- A **checkout** is a page where you complete your purchase by entering your credit card and delivery address details.

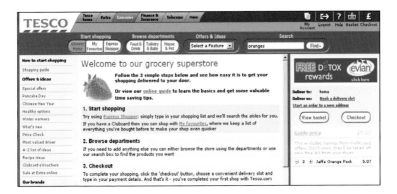

Take a look around by following some links on the site. It's just the same as looking at the other sites you have been visiting in previous chapters.

Browsing and finding items

You shop online in just the same way as you do in a shop – by browsing what they have on offer and choosing what you want. Start to shop by finding and selecting the items you would like to buy. You can do this by either clicking on a suitable link or using a mini-search engine on the site. In this exercise, we'll use both methods to find and select some fruit to buy.

Step 1 Find the **Groceries** link on the left-hand side of the page and click on it once. If this is the first time you've visited, you'll be taken to the **Registration** page where Tesco will first take some details about you before you are allowed to do some shopping.

Step 2 After registering, you are taken to the **Groceries** page. Notice the little search engine on the top right-hand side of the page. You can find specific items using this search engine (which limits its search to only the Tesco website).

Step 3 Type in 'oranges' and click once on the **Find** button. The search engine returns a long list of items available at Tesco containing the word 'orange,' ranging from orange juice to orange marmalade.

Step 4 Fortunately, the page also lists some 'shelves' that you can look at. Find this list (located just above the search results) and click once on the link marked 'Oranges'. This now brings up a list of different types of oranges available.

Viewing and selecting items

Step 1 To see a picture of a listed item, simply click once on it to open a small window with a photo. Close the window when you are done by clicking once on the **X** icon found on the top right-hand corner of the window.

Step 2 To select an item to buy, click once on the **add** button next to it. Go ahead and click once on the **add** button near the Jaffa Orange Pack link.

Step 3 You can specify the number of items you wish to buy by clicking on the **plus** or **minus** buttons and then clicking on the **add** button.

Step 4 Select more items to buy if you wish.

Step 5 When you've finished shopping, click once on **Basket** or **View Basket** to see a list of items you've selected.

Step 6 If you are happy with the number and cost amount shown, move on to the next step.

Paying for your purchases

This is a simple step-by-step process. Simply read through each stage, fill in the information asked for and move on to the next stage.

Don't worry **if you make a mistake**

If you miss out something essential when you are filling in details and then move on to the next page, the site will simply send you back. It will probably put a red * next to the things you need to fill in.

You are not committed to your purchases until you have completed all the information, including your credit or debit card details, and pressed **Confirm**.

Step 1 Click once on the **Checkout** link or button.

Step 2 You will be taken to the page where you can select a delivery slot from what is available. Click once on one of the slots to select a delivery time that suits you. Check that you are happy with the cost of delivery.

Step 3 You'll then be taken to the secure checkout page where you'll be asked for your credit or debit card details. Fill in the information requested.

Security tip

Always remember to look out for the little security icon on the bottom right-hand corner of your desktop whenever you make an online financial transaction.

Step 4 Before you click on the **Confirm** button to send your order, check the **Order Summary** details to confirm that you understand and are happy with any charges that will be made.

3. Order Summary			
Product description	**Quantity**	**Item price**	**Total price**
▸ Show only item summary	7	-	£10.33
Loose Oranges Class 1	1	£0.19	£0.19
Jaffa Orange Pack	6	£1.69	£10.14
(change basket ▸)		**Subtotal of all items:**	£10.33
		Service Charge:	£5.99
		Total to pay*:	**£16.32**
*This is a guide price only. Product prices may change in store between now and when your order is delivered.			

Step 5 Once you are happy that everything is correct, press **Confirm**.

Step 6 It is a good idea to print a copy of the order and keep it for future reference.

That's it! All you have to do now is wait for your purchases to arrive at your doorstep!

It's a big wide world

Do remember that the internet is international, so you may find yourself on a non-UK-based site. When you check your delivery arrangements, make sure you take a look at the delivery time and where the goods are coming from.

What else can I buy?

The same principles apply to anything you want to buy online, so you can buy almost any product you might want:

- **foods** – especially useful for unusual items, such as allergen-free options, that you can't find in your local supermarket;

- **household goods or furniture** – especially awkward or bulky items that stores will usually expect you to take away just because some customers can carry huge boxes to a huge Volvo;

- **books** – to find a much broader range than your local bookshop;

- **health supplements** – of every type imaginable;
- **clothes** – difficult-to-find items can usually be found on the net.

You can also access all sorts of services online:

- **insurance** – for everything from home to holidays, including online quotes;
- **banking** – you can organise your finances, pay bills and transfer money;
- **holidays** – a huge resource for holidays of all kinds, including last-minute bookings;
- **travel arrangements** – such as trains and planes.

The online world is the biggest shopping mall you could ever imagine!

Your reminder box

- Use reputable sites or check them out carefully.
- Register on the site using your e-mail and a password.
- Only give financial details if the site tells you it is a secure, encrypted transaction.
- Select your goods, which will collect in the **Shopping basket**.
- Check you only have what you want, then proceed to the **Checkout**.
- Decide on your delivery arrangements and make sure you are happy with the cost.
- Fill in your credit or debit card details.
- Confirm your purchase.

Chapter 9
Finding Information

By now, you are really getting adept at using the net, so you can spread your wings even further and start to look at sites of interest to you on every possible topic. The internet is the biggest, most impressive library you could wish for.

Think about what you learnt in Chapter 7 about using search engines:

- Go to your chosen search engine; we used **www.yahoo.co.uk** and **www.google.co.uk**.

- Type in the topic you are interested in (for more tips, look back at page 86) and click on **Search**.

- Look through the list and click on the one that interests you.

We have selected a few specific topics that might be of interest, but once you have mastered the techniques, you can apply them to anything you want to find out.

Family history

When it comes to researching your family history, the internet beats every visit to a library or government office you've made, hands down. You can obtain online and hard copies of certificates of birth, death and marriage; do searches on names (especially unusual ones); and, with luck, even find a relative or two you did not know you had.

Google it

If you have an unusual family name you could start simply by 'Googling' it – that is, typing the name into the Google search engine, and seeing what comes up. You could be surprised.

Try finding other sites by Googling various words and phrases like:

'researching your family tree' uk

> **FAQ**
>
> You'll find this on lots of sites and it stands for Frequently Asked Questions. It will offer you a list of information in question-and-answer format.

Find the records

The more sophisticated way to go about it, though, would be to visit sites where you can obtain and view actual records.

www.familyrecords.gov.uk is an excellent place to start. From this site you can obtain copies of birth, marriage and death certificates, for a very small fee. The site also has links to other sites that can help.

One such site is the General Register Office **www.gro.gov.uk**, which has an extensive archive of statutory records dating to the beginning of civil registration in 1837 and can help with research going even further back in time. You can even make applications for overseas birth, death or marriage certificates here.

The people behind Friends Reunited, the hugely successful website for locating old school friends, have now come up with Genes Reunited, which could help locate relatives. You'll find it at **www.genesreunited.co.uk**.

> **Tip**
>
> Always try the free sites first – you could be surprised at how much information people are more than happy to share on the net.

Travel

The internet has truly revolutionised the world of travel by making accessible to all the means to plan, shop around for and pay for journeys home and abroad.

Start local

To start with, why not find out about places of local interest such as a stately home or park. A quick search on the internet will bring up websites with detailed information regarding opening times, accessibility, etc. about a place or site you'd like to visit.

Useful websites for the local tourist include **www.tourist-information-uk.com**, which has links to the websites of major tourist attractions in England and Wales.

Plan a journey

Now see if you can plan a train journey. For UK travel, you can plan your journey and book train tickets at:

www.nationalrail.co.uk

www.trainline.com

or plan your road trip at:

www.rac.co.uk

www.theaa.com

from the comfort of your home. You can also get journey planners from the RAC site. Or, if you want a street map of the place you are visiting – whether it is around the corner or at the other side of the country – simply go to:

www.multimap.com

www.streetmap.co.uk

and key in the postcode. So easy!

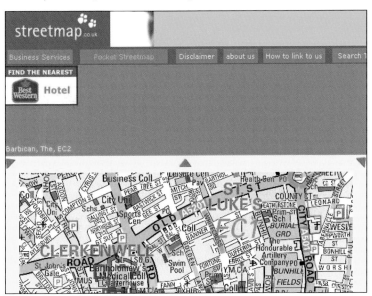

Take a virtual journey

Now think a bit further afield and think about your next holiday. Start your journey by making an initial virtual visit to your proposed destination. Or you could look up somewhere you know already so you can judge the quality of the information on offer.

- For a pleasant online jaunt through different cities of the world, for example, visit website:

www.virtourist.com

- The Lonely Planet site at **www.lonelyplanet.co.uk** has excellent online guides for several destinations.

- You could also search the internet for photos and write-ups on various destinations simply by keying in the name of the destination.

- Most travel companies have their own destination guides on their sites, so visit people such as Thomas Cook on **www.thomascook.com**, Airtours on **www.airtours.co.uk** or other travel companies.

Find a good deal

Once you've made up your mind where to go, planning your journey couldn't be easier. Now you need to decide who you are going to use to plan your holiday: you can go to a tour operator or put the whole thing together yourself by booking the individual elements separately (although if you are a newcomer, the first option may be preferable).

The internet really comes into its own when shopping for travel deals. There are hundreds of sites that allow you to find, book and pay for holidays, which often works out cheaper than using high-street travel agents. Many well-known holiday companies will often offer cheaper products via their websites.

Some well-known sites include:

www. opodo.co.uk

www.ebookers.com

www.lastminute.com

When shopping for holiday bargains, keep in mind the commonsense precautions discussed on page 91. When you are booking through a travel agent or on the phone, you would make sure the company are reputable and ABTA-bonded; make sure you do the same for online firms.

Health information

The internet is bursting at the seams with health advice. There isn't a better place to look, especially if you are researching a rare condition or wish to read and share first-person accounts of specific health experiences.

Use reputable sources

Good places to start are official or accredited sites such as:

www.nhs.uk

www.patient.co.uk

> ### Remember, sites are not regulated
>
> As always, keep your sceptic's glasses on when visiting non-accredited sites – there is a great deal of misinformation on the net. Do not allow yourself to be drawn in to sites that are alarmist or do not provide you with reliable data. Stick with reputable information providers and you will be fine.

Support organisations and self-help groups

You will also find that most support organisations have their own websites, such as:

www.arc.org.uk

www.parkinsons.org.uk

www.diabetes.org.uk

www.cancerresearchuk.org

www.breastcancer.org

www.bhf.org.uk

Just type the address in the Address Bar, as usual, and use the links to find your way around the information on their sites.

Education

If you need to further your education, learn a new skill or simply take on a new hobby, the internet can be incredibly useful. There is a lot on offer, ranging from online courses, both free and paid, to information about how to find and enrol for normal classroom-based courses.

Learning a new skill

If you are learning a new skill, check out the internet for the hundreds or free tutorials you will find on almost any subject. For example, Barnes and Noble offers free online courses ranging from PC care to yoga. You can find a list of these at:

university.barnesandnoble.com

Almost all learning institutes now have an official website, which is always a good place to start when researching a specific course. The website of your local university is always the university name followed by .ac.uk, so:

www.exeter.ac.uk

www.kingston.ac.uk

www.reading.ac.uk

www.lancaster.ac.uk

Your local colleges and evening-class venues are likely to have all their information online. If you want a printed prospectus, you will probably be able to order one from the site, or e-mail them with any queries about the course or the college.

LearnDirect and Hot Courses have online catalogues at:

www.learndirect.co.uk

www.hotcourses.com

Getting down to detail

Don't forget that you can use your search engine to be as specific as you want. If you want to find out about anything from iguanas to igneous rocks, just type the keyword into your search engine and follow the links.

Local support networks

The internet can be an excellent tool for quickly locating support groups dealing with various issues. Start by running a search with the name of the topic you'd like help with, together with your town or region name as keywords. Be sure to add the keyword 'uk' to restrict the search to the UK alone.

Some websites, such as:

www.ukselfhelp.info

have lists of support groups that could help you in your search. Local Authority websites will also have links to pages with lists of support groups available in your area. For example, the London Borough of Bromley site:

www.bromley.gov.uk

lists over 100 local support groups on its Advice and Local Support Groups page that can be accessed from its Community Organisations link on the Community People and Living page.

Advisory & Local Support Groups - A-Z Listing

- 'The Centre' - Cotmandene Crescent
- Abacus: The Cancer Self Help Support Group
- Action for Victims of Medical Accidents (AVMA)
- Action in Communities (formerly Welcome Project for Refugees)
- Addictions Anonymous
- Age Concern Bromley
- Alcoholics Anonymous
- Allergy UK
- Alzheimer's Society - Bromley
- Association of Teachers of Lipreading to Adults
- Barnardo's Apex Project
- Beckenham & Penge Citizens Advice Bureau
- Beckenham and Bromley Twins Club
- BEE - Bromley Eating Experience
- Bereavement Centre for the Borough of Bromley
- Bexley and Bromley Citizen Advocacy
- Biggin Hill & District National Childbirth Trust
- Both Parents Forever
- British Cardiac Patients Association - Zipper Club

- Gordon House Association
- Groves House Toy Library
- Help Desk Service - Bromley Magistrates' Court
- Home-Start Bromley
- I-Care Day Centre Trust Ltd
- I.A. The Ileostomy & Internal Pouch Support Group
- I B S Treatment Programme
- Independent Housing Ombudsman
- JOBMATCH
- Josef's House
- Kent Association for the Blind
- Keston Care Group
- LATCH Project
- Leukaemia Research Fund
- Life Education Centres - Bromley
- Lifelink
- Lupus UK (South London)
- Macmillan Cancer Relief
- Manic Depression Fellowship

News

With the internet you need never be left in the dark again! All major newspapers and TV channels have online versions, and there's plenty more in the form of online newsletters and specialist news websites. Try doing a Google search on the keywords 'news uk' to see what I mean.

Some suggestions to get you started:

news.bbc.co.uk

www.reuters.co.uk

www.sky.com

www.independent.co.uk

www.telegraph.co.uk

THE INDEPENDENT — ONLINE EDITION

With Tiscali, everyone in the land can afford Broadband!

News
UK
Europe
World
Business
Media
People

Sport
Cricket
Fishing
General
Golf
Motor Racing
Olympics
Rugby League
Rugby Union
Sports Politics
Tennis
Football

Comment
Leading Articles
Letters
Commentators
Podium
Regular Columnists

Education
News
Business Schools
Careers Advice
Gap Year

TOP STORIES

100 Labour MPs back reform
Pressure on Tony Blair to modernise the voting system increased as it emerged that almost 100 Labour MPs, including several cabinet ministers, support electoral reform

· **Readers letters on vote reform**

Galloway denies fresh allegations

A US Senate committee probing corruption in the UN oil-for-food programme says that the British MP George Galloway was given options on millions of barrels of oil from Saddam Hussein's regime

Nuclear power may be the only way, says chief scientist
Britain may need one more generation of nuclear power stations to fight against climate change, the Government's chief scientific adviser says

EDITOR'S CHOICE

Safe as houses
Helping people who can't pay their rent

Janet Street-Porter
The snobbish delusions of a dreary mall P

Debra Winger
On life away from Hollywood

Adrian Hamilton
Why Blair didn't go to Moscow for VE Day P

Locked Out
65,000 Indians on the wrong side of the fence

John Walsh
Tales of the City P

Florence Nightingale
Seen in a new light

DAY IN A PAGE

Sun | Mon | Tue | Wed | Thu | Fri | Sat

Sport

Everything a sports fan will ever need can be found easily on the net:

- sports news;
- scores and results;
- video replays;
- event tickets;
- team websites.

You name it, the internet's got it.

For sports news, try:

msn.skysports.com

news.bbc.co.uk/sport

Yahoo! UK's sports page on **uk.sports.yahoo.com**

Look up your local club on your search engine, or take a guess at its website address :

www.manutd.com

www.arsenal.com

www.northamptonsaints.co.uk

www.beesprohockey.com

www.glosccc.co.uk

The governing body is also likely to have a site, which you can find with your search engine:

www.rfu.com

www.mcc.org

You are probably getting the idea that, with a little surfing, you can find whatever you want.

Events, culture, arts and theatre

You can readily get access to local, national and international information on the arts, entertainment, heritage and leisure activities on the internet.

Many events have websites that give details such as performance times, prices and availability on the internet. You can also beat entrance queues by purchasing online tickets to events.

Most events are listed on local websites, so it is worth having a specific place in mind before you start a search and going straight to that site:

www.royalexchange.co.uk

www.paviliontheatre.co.uk

Some towns and cities have specific information sites:

www.officiallondontheatre.co.uk

www.readingarts.com

www.mycardiff.net

Brit Info Net, found at **www.britinfo.net**, is a useful site for finding out contact details for local theatres and cinemas, leisure and sports centres and social clubs.

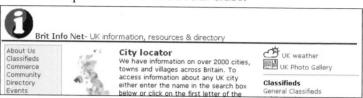

Hobbies

As a resource tool for hobbies, you cannot beat the internet. Whether your hobby is building model ships or gardening, you can find anything from inspiration to tutorials, local groups, supplies, forums and competitions online.

Stuck for inspiration? For ideas, just do a search using the word 'hobbies' as a keyword and see what comes up.

Directory sites can be particularly useful here. These sites list links under different categories that can make it easier to locate information. Visit:

www.ukdirectory.co.uk

and find the Lifestyle link. I was able to find some pretty good listings for a wide variety of hobbies.

The rest is up to you! Use the name of your hobby as a keyword to search for more information.

Your reminder box

- Search engines are invaluable for finding information on the net.

- Find information on anything from aardvarks to zeitgeist.

- As always, use reputable sites so you can rely on the information you find.

Chapter 10

Get In Touch

The internet offers dozens of ways in which you can get in touch with other people. Whether you want 'real time' conversations with friends, or to share opinions with like-minded individuals, or simply to learn about other people's experiences, you can be sure that – short of popping your head over the fence – the internet is the simplest, cheapest and most convenient way to do it.

Chatting online

An online conversation taking place in a virtual 'room' is called a chat. Chatting takes place in real time and anyone with access to the chat room can read the messages that have been typed in and respond to them. There are two ways to chat: a safe way and a risky way.

Let's dismiss the risky way first. An open chat room is accessible to anyone. People participating are identified by a username, which can be created before accessing the room. Usernames usually do not have any relation to a person's real name. Because of the anonymity they afford, chat rooms are awash with individuals who have good reason to keep their real identities hidden. Stay away. There are far safer ways to get in touch with like-minded individuals.

Secure online chatting

A number of ISPs and online companies offer safe online chatting services that allow you to communicate with others over the internet in real time. This is very much like speaking to someone on the telephone, only your conversation is typed rather than spoken. Communication is secure because you are ever only in contact with people you know. As with a phone with a conference facility, you can also chat in a group.

MSN's Messenger is a popular secure online chatting service. All you need is a hotmail e-mail address and the messaging software, both of which can be easily obtained (free) from **www.msn.co.uk** and **messenger.msn.co.uk**. The software download link has simple instructions on how to install the software and run the messaging program. Anyone you wish to chat to will also have to download and install the same messaging software.

To chat, exchange your hotmail e-mail address with the people you wish to communicate with and you are ready to go.

Step 1   Go to **www.msn.co.uk**, sign into your hotmail account and go to **My MSN**, then to **Actions**.

Step 2   Choose **Add a contact**, type in the e-mail address of the person you would like to chat to and press **Next**. You have then chosen to be able to talk to them online.

Step 3   MSN will e-mail them to tell them you have added them to your contacts list and ask them if they want to add you to their list. If they do, then you can talk to them online. If they don't, they can either block you or delete and block you.

This list of e-mail addresses forms your **Contacts** list. Whenever anyone in your list is online, Messenger will let you know so you can have a chat, if you wish.

Another popular and very similar online chatting service is Yahoo!'s Messenger, which can be found on **uk.messenger.yahoo.com**.

Message boards

Most websites have a message board, or forum, where members can place short messages regarding a certain topic. This is called **posting**. Once you have made a post, other members can read your post and make their own posts in response to yours, creating a chain of related messages called a **discussion thread**.

This is a safe way to communicate with others, as most message boards have strict rules of conduct and a moderator who enforces them. Some message boards, for example, do not allow members to use the board to advertise products. Members who break the rules can be banned from the boards. Unmoderated boards do exist but are still a safer online communication medium than chat rooms.

To find message boards, visit your favourite website and look out for links such as **Forums** or **Have your say**.

The picture below shows the I-Village travel message board found at **messageboards.ivillage.co.uk/iv-uktrtravel**:

General Discussions		Post a message	Create a poll	Folder Outline
Subject	Started by	No. of Msgs		Most Recent
☿ mossies......	suzcat	5 new		6-Jul
Half price luggage??	ivillager	5 new		6-Jul
keeping your stuff safe	ivyblue	2 new		5-Jul
? Help in Cyprus Please	gal_sammy1	1 new		3-Jul
Anyone experienced Turkey?	loobylou79	8 new		1-Jul
? Majorca	girly_girl25	5 new		1-Jul
⊗ British people and sunny weather	madcow42	4 new		30-Jun
▦ turkey	partygal	2 new		30-Jun
▣ Travel Writing	ivill_christina	1 new		30-Jun

When registering for membership on a message board, you might be asked to select a username, which will be used to identify you to other forum members online.

Some message boards like you to use your real name, but commonly a username will have no relationship to your real name so that only the message board moderator will know who you really are, having taken your details when you registered.

My tip

It's a good idea to have more than one e-mail address – one for friends and family, a second one for discussion boards, registering on sites, etc.

Newsgroups

Newsgroups developed before widespread use of e-mails and web pages, when the best way to communicate on the internet was to post a text message on an electronic bulletin board.

Newsgroups have some similarities with message boards, as newsgroup members too, will communicate by reading and responding to other members' online posts. However, newsgroups are a rather more sophisticated form of communication because they offer many more features than can be found on a simple message board. An example of one is shown below.

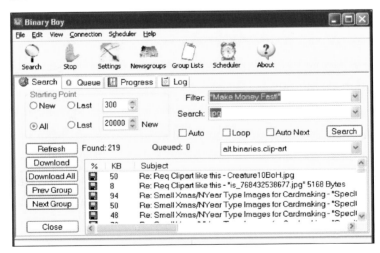

To use these features, you need to download and install special software, called a **newsreader** and there are several newsreader programs available on the internet. Apart from allowing you to find, read and respond to posts, they come with several other features:

- an attachments feature that allows you to share files with other members;

- picture gallery and in-built image viewers so that members can share photos;

- encryption to keep all communication confidential;

- password protection to restrict your communication to members only;

- scanning of downloads from the site for viruses to guarantee safety and security.

There are thousands of different newsgroups available online, dealing with an incredibly varied numbers of different topics. One of the oldest collections of newsgroups forms an entity called Usenet at

www.usenet.com

which today also remains one of the world's largest. The Usenet and Google (**groups.google.co.uk**) newsgroup home pages are good places to start your search for an online community with your subject of interest.

Exchange of messages on a newsgroup is usually via text, but increasingly, other electronic material such as movies, pictures, music files, and programs can also be shared among users, making it an excellent medium for exchanging computer files and documents.

When you are sending information to a newsgroup, it can be on one of 10 topic groups. The name of the file will end in a few letters that tell you what the message is about.

- **alt**.: any topic at all

- **biz**.: business products, services, reviews
- **comp**.: hardware, software, consumer information
- **humanities**.: fine art, literature, philosophy
- **misc**.: employment, health and much more
- **news**.: information about Usenet News
- **rec**.: games, hobbies, sports
- **sci**.: applied science, social science
- **soc**.: social issues, culture
- **talk**.: current issues and debates.

As with message boards, newsgroups can have rules and codes of conduct for everyone's safety and convenience. Always take time to familiarise yourself with a group's rules. Avoid posting private e-mail messages on newsgroups and be sure to check the spelling and grammar on your post.

How to post and read on newsgroups

Many newsgroups do not need you to download any special software; they work very much like a message board. Just find the newsgroup on the internet, register and log on to the site if you need to, and start reading the messages.

A newsgroup message list will look like this:

A newsgroup post will look like this:

If you'd like to respond to a post, just click on the link that says **Post a follow-up to this message**. A new window appears that allows you to type in your response. When you've finished, click on the **Submit** button to send your message, which will eventually appear as part of the topic's thread.

Newsgroups that use newsreader software will have a download link where the program can be found, as well as instructions on how to install and use it. You can download a newsreader program from the News Rover site at **www.newsrover.com/ usenet.htm**, which also has an excellent tutorial on newsgroups in general.

Your reminder box

• Avoid open chat rooms.

• Use secure online chatting with MSN.

• Post information on message boards and see if other people respond.

• Use newsgroups to get in touch with other people on a specific topic.

Conclusion

What Next?

The most important thing about using a computer is confidence. Relax, enjoy it, try things one at a time as you feel ready and you'll soon feel as at home on the screen as you do in the library.

If you have worked through this book, you'll have enough information to be able to find your way around quite easily, and hopefully will have been cured of your nervousness of computers. That means you are now ready to go off on your own and keep expanding your knowledge.

The internet has revolutionised the way the world works, and there are so many benefits to be had from knowing your way around – from being able to contact your grandchildren in a café in Thailand to saving you traipsing around the supermarket, booking your holiday or finding out the very latest information on health issues.

Plus there's always something new around the corner and you are in the best position to find out about them and benefit from them. Here are some more things you can do on your computer, and new developments you might be interested in:

- **Your own website:** These are remarkably easy to create as most computers will have a program that helps you build a site and get it on the net. There well also be a step-by-step on-screen wizard program to guide you.

- **Voice-activated computer programs:** No more tedious typing! Current programs are still rather cumbersome and error-prone, but they are getting better all the time so it may not be so long before we start to use them every day.

- **Web cams:** You can already buy cameras and programs that link to your e-mail so you can not only write to your relatives in Australia, but you can also see them, too.

- **Voice telephone calls over the internet:** Imagine being able to call anywhere in the world for the cost of a local telephone call!

- **Computer TV:** For those planning to jump ship and emigrate, here's one less thing to worry about – you can take your TV programmes with you! Unless this was the reason you were leaving in the first place ...

Feeling ambitious with your digital camera?

How would you like to show off photos of your project with friends? Why not simply use an online photo album service to display your digital photos online? You can control access to your photos by setting a username and password. Two online photos hosting sites are **www.mysnaps.com** and **photos.yahoo.com**.

Computer Terms you Might Come Across

Use this section to remind yourself of essential terms if you need to, or to help you understand computer terminology you'll come across as you get more proficient on the internet.

Bandwidth A measure of the speed of a link between computers in Kilo, Mega or Giga bits per second. A dial-up modem can give speeds of about 50Kbps. Broadband connection speeds range from 256Kbps to 1 or 3Mbps.

Broadband You connect to the internet via a phone line, usually what's called a dial-up connection. If you have broadband, you can send and receive more data more quickly, and talk on the phone at the same time.

CD Short for Compact Disk. High-capacity computer disks for storing data. To read data from a CD you need a CD drive.

CD burner A special type of CD drive that can write on to as well as read data from a CD. Ordinary CD drives only read CD data.

CD-ROM Short for Compact Disk Read Only Memory. The Read Only bit means that once data has been recorded on them, it can only be read or played, but not altered or edited (writeable CDs on the other hand, can be used over and over again).

Click Quickly pressing and releasing the left-hand mouse button once.

Cyberspace The virtual world created by the internet.

Desktop The display on a computer screen that represents your real desktop.

Double-click Quickly pressing and releasing the left-hand mouse button twice.

Download Transferring online data on to your PC.

Drive A slot on a computer where portable storage devices such as floppies or CD-ROMs are inserted.

DVD Short for Digital Versatile Disk. A high-capacity disk that is used to store movies.

FAQ Short for Frequently Asked Questions and found on many websites so they don't have to keep replying to the same queries.

File An electronic document stored on a computer.

Firewall A barrier on an internet connection that prevents unauthorised access to a computer or network. Firewalls monitor connection attempts to your computer and block any suspect ones.

Floppy A portable storage device used to store computer data. Floppies are inserted into floppy disk drives.

Folder A collection of computer files grouped together so you can find them easily, just like putting sheets of paper into a cardboard file.

Hacker Someone who tries to gain unauthorised access to your computer.

Hard disk A fixed magnetic disk used to store data on the computer.

Hardware The physical components of a computer.

Hyperlink A link on a website that you can click on to send you to another part of the website or to another website.

Icon A small picture representation of a computer file, link or program. You can double-click on an icon to get to the program.

ISP Short for internet Service Provider. A company that provides access to the internet to individuals or businesses.

Keyword A word used to search for information on a search engine.

Link A link on a website that you can click on to send you to another part of the website or to another website.

Mail server A specialised computer that manages e-mail. Mail servers work like a virtual post office, storing, forwarding and sorting e-mail arriving from the internet.

Memory stick A high-capacity portable storage device used to store computer data. Memory sticks are inserted into the USB port of a computer.

Modem A device that converts digital data into a form that can be transported over an analogue telephone line and vice versa.

Mouse A hand-held device that you move on your real desktop while the movements are mirrored by a pointer on the computer screen. You click the mouse button to activate a program or link.

Network A group of computers linked together. The internet is the largest public network in the world.

Offline Not connected to the internet.

Online Connected to the internet.

Operating system Special software that manages programs and applications on a computer.

PC Short for Personal Computer.

Port A socket on a computer to connect cables to devices such as printers and scanners.

Processor Also called microprocessor or Central Processing Unit (CPU), this is a silicon chip that controls the processes of a computer. How much data the processor can process at a time is measured in megahertz (MHz).

RAM Short for Random Access Memory. The memory available for computing processes when a computer is switched on. The more RAM a computer has, the larger the number of different processes it can run at the same time. RAM is measured in Megabytes (MB).

Right-click Quickly pressing and releasing the right-hand side mouse button once.

Search engine A program found on the internet that searches for all documents and websites that contain a certain keyword.

Server A high-capacity computer specialised to perform a specific function. Types of servers include mail servers that manage e-mail on the internet, and web servers that store web pages.

Software The programs on a computer.

Spam The internet equivalent of junk mail. Unsolicited e-mail from an unknown contact.

Surfing Visiting web pages and sites on the net.

Surfer A website visitor.

URL Short for Uniform (or Universal) Resource Locator – a complicated name for a web address.

USB port Short for Universal Serial Bus. A special socket used to plug in devices such as printers.

Virus A program that is inserted into your computer without your consent and with malicious intent. A virus interferes with the proper workings of your computer.

Web The internet, cyperspace, the world wide web, the net.

Web browser A computer program used to view web pages on the internet, like Microsoft's Internet Explorer, or Netscape Navigator.

Web page A document displaying information on the internet.

Website A group of related web pages.

Index